# A Journey
# with Luke

*The 50 Day Bible Challenge*

This collection © 2015 Marek P. Zabriskie

Individual essays are the property of the authors.

All rights reserved.

ISBN: 978-0-88028-429-5

Printed in USA

Second printing, 2016

Forward Movement

# A Journey
# with Luke

## *The 50 Day Bible Challenge*

Edited by Marek P. Zabriskie

FORWARD MOVEMENT
Cincinnati, Ohio

# Preface

The Bible Challenge began as a simple idea: to encourage daily reading of scripture. Simple ideas can bring forth great change.

Developing a daily spiritual discipline or practice is crucial for all Christians who wish to be faithful followers of Jesus. Saint Augustine and many other great Christians have written about the power of reading the Bible quietly on our own. There is no other book in the world that can so transform the human heart, motivate the human spirit, and give us the mind that was in Christ Jesus himself.

The Bible remains the world's best-selling book year after year. However, Episcopalians, Roman Catholics, and other mainline Christians often do not read it. Church historian and author Diana Butler Bass reports that among the 22,000 Christian groups and denominations in the United States, Episcopalians are the best-educated group but drop to nearly last when it comes to biblical literacy.

The goal of The Bible Challenge is to help individuals develop a lifelong, daily spiritual discipline of reading the Bible so that their lives may be constantly transformed and renewed. Studies reveal that prayerfully engaging scripture is the best way for Christians to grow in their faith and love of Jesus.

More than 250,000 persons in 2,500 churches in over forty countries are now participating in The Bible Challenge. We continue our partnership with Forward Movement with this new series—a focus on reading one book of the Bible over a fifty-day period. This book joins *A Journey with Matthew* and *A Journey with Mark* as the third book in the series. This Bible Challenge series is an ideal resource for individuals, churches, and dioceses during the Easter season or any time of the year.

Regular engagement with the Bible develops a strong Christian faith, enhances our experience of worship, and helps to create a more committed, articulate, and contagious Christian. This is exactly what the world needs today.

With prayers and blessings for your faithful Bible reading,

The Rev. Marek P. Zabriskie
Founder of The Bible Challenge
Director of the Center for Biblical Studies
www.thecenterforbiblicalstudies.org
Rector of St. Thomas' Episcopal Church
Fort Washington, Pennsylvania

*A Journey with Luke*

# How to Read the Bible Prayerfully

Welcome to The 50 Day Bible Challenge. We are delighted that you are interested in reading God's life-transforming Word from the Gospel of Luke. It will change and enrich your life. Here are some suggestions to consider as you get started:

- You can begin The 50 Day Bible Challenge at any time of the year that you desire. It works especially well for the fifty days of Eastertide, beginning on Easter Day. It also could be read during Lent, beginning on the Sunday before Ash Wednesday.

- Each day has a manageable amount of reading, a meditation, a question or two, and a prayer, written by a host of wonderful authors.

- We suggest that you try to read the Bible each day. It is a great spiritual discipline to establish.

- If, however, you need more than fifty days to read through the Gospel of Luke, we support you in moving at the pace that works best for you.

- Many Bible Challenge participants read the Bible using their iPad, iPhone, Kindle, or Nook, or listen to the Bible on CDs or on a mobile device using Audio.com, faithcomesthroughhearing.org, or Pandora radio. Find what works for you.

- Our website, www.forwardmovement.org, offers many resources for learning more about the Bible and engaging in scripture. In addition, you can find a list of resources at www.thecenterforbiblicalresources.org. The center also offers a Read the Bible in a Year program and reading plans for the New Testament, Psalms, and Proverbs.

- Because the Bible is not a newspaper, it is best to read it with a reverent spirit. We advocate a devotional approach to reading the Bible, rather than reading it as a purely intellectual or academic exercise.

- Before reading the Bible, take a moment of silence to put yourself in the presence of God. We then invite you to read this prayer written by Archbishop Thomas Cranmer.

  *Blessed Lord, who has caused all holy scriptures to be written for our learning: Grant us to hear them, read, mark, learn, and inwardly digest them, that we may embrace and ever hold fast the blessed hope of everlasting life, which you have given us in our Savior Jesus Christ; who lives and reigns with you and the Holy Spirit, one God, for ever and ever.* Amen.

- Consider using the ancient monastic practice of *lectio divina*. In this form of Bible reading, you read the text and then meditate on a portion of it—be it a verse or two or even a single word. Mull over the words and their meaning. Then offer a prayer to God based on what you have read and how it has made you feel or what it has caused you to ponder. Listen in silence for God to respond to your prayer.

- We encourage you to read in the morning, if possible, so that your prayerful reading may spiritually enliven the rest of your day. If you cannot read in the morning, read when you can later in the day. Try to carve out a regular time for your daily reading.

- One way to hold yourself accountable to reading God's Word is to form a group within your church or community. By participating in The 50 Day Bible Challenge together, you can support one another in your reading, discuss the Bible passages, ask questions, and share how God's Word is transforming your life.

- If you do not want to join a group, you may wish to invite a friend or family member or two to share The 50 Day Bible Challenge with you.

- Put a notice in your church newsletter that you are starting a group to participate in The 50 Day Bible Challenge. Invite others to join you and to gather regularly to discuss the readings, ask questions, and share how it is transforming your life. Visit the Center for Biblical Resources website to see more suggestions about how churches can participate in The Bible Challenge.

- If you form a Bible Challenge group, consider holding a gathering or meal to celebrate your spiritual accomplishment.

- Have fun and find spiritual peace and the joy that God desires for you in your daily reading. The goal of the

Center for Biblical Studies is to help you discover God's wisdom and to create a lifelong spiritual practice of daily Bible reading so that God may guide you through each day of your life.

- If you find reading the entire Bible and being part of The Bible Challenge to be a blessing in your life, then we strongly encourage you to share the blessing. Invite several friends or family members to participate in The Bible Challenge.

- Once you've finished one complete reading of the Bible, start over and do it again. God may speak differently to you in each reading. Follow the example of US President John Adams, who read through the Bible each year during his adult life. We highly advocate this practice.

- After participating in The 50 Day Bible Challenge, you will be more equipped to support and mentor others in reading the Bible.

We are thrilled that you are participating in The Bible Challenge. May God richly bless you as you prayerfully engage the scriptures each day.

# An Introduction to the Gospel of Luke

I first fell in love with the Gospel of Luke shortly after graduating from college. I was headed to France with dreams of becoming fluent in French, hoping to study philosophy at the Sorbonne or theology at the Institute Catholique. Before moving to Paris, I had arranged to work in the *vendange,* the French grape harvest, in a little village outside Saumur.

A professor of philosophy and mentor from Emory University gave me a small red book as a farewell gift. It contained the four gospels and the Acts of the Apostles in French. I carried it with me and began reading it faithfully, digesting the stories of Jesus, his teachings, miracles, and parables as told by the four evangelists and reading in Acts about how the Church began.

I became especially enamored with the Gospel of Luke. A master storyteller, Luke wrote like a journalist. I had been an editor at my college newspaper, and Luke's descriptive writing style captivated me and made the stories about Jesus come to life.

Legend has it that Luke was an artist and painted as well as wrote. He was said to have interviewed eyewitnesses to the life, ministry, death, and resurrection of Jesus. In this sense, he was a journalist. Some traditions say that Luke not only met and interviewed Jesus' mother Mary, but he also painted her portrait. This portrait is known as "The Black Madonna," and it is Poland's most treasured sacred relic.

Luke was also said to have been a physician. It is believed that he was Paul's traveling companion. Luke uses the most sophisticated Greek found in the New Testament. He was clearly the most learned among the New Testament writers. On several occasions he uses precise and unusual medical terms, offering evidence of his training in medicine.

Luke's training and experience as a physician allowed him to see and appreciate things in Jesus' ministry that did not strike the other evangelists to the same extent.

Most of Jesus' ministry begins with his senses. He looks and he sees. He listens and he hears. His eyes wide open and his ears alert, Jesus sees and hears the pressing needs of those around him, and he responds compassionately. Time and again, Jesus physically heals those in need around him. Luke's Gospel conveys more healing stories than any of the other three gospels. Luke portrays Jesus as a compassionate healer. In fact, if there is one word that best summarizes Luke's depiction of Jesus, it is "compassionate."

Jesus' compassion, however, extends beyond those who were physically and mentally impaired or suffering. It extends to the poor and outcast. Jesus includes marginalized people in his conversations, healings, meals, and ministry that other Jews and Romans of his day exclude. He constantly draws the circle of God's love wider. While others are concerned about whom to exclude, Jesus expands the circle to demonstrate how God's love, grace, and forgiveness know no bounds.

The poor are constantly on Jesus' mind, as evidenced in Luke's Gospel. Scholars believe that the Gospel of Mark was the first to be written. It is the shortest and most concise telling of the story of Jesus' life and ministry. Matthew's Gospel was the second. It elaborates on many of the stories and adds details and events like a birth narrative, which is not found in Mark. Luke's account is even longer. He adds three parables found nowhere else in the gospels—the parables of the prodigal son, the good Samaritan, and the unjust judge. All three are stories about mercy and forgiveness, justice, and love. They exude compassion and mercy, the defining characteristics of Jesus as revealed by Luke.

In Matthew's Gospel, Jesus offers his finest sermon—the Sermon on the Mount, in which Jesus lays out his definitive teachings in a sermon of poetic beauty and unsurpassed wisdom. Scholars believe that the Sermon on the Mount was actually a series of Jesus' sermons strung together like a "greatest hits" of preaching.

In Luke's Gospel, Jesus offers a similar discourse but with two very distinct differences. In Luke's Gospel, Jesus does not stand at the brow of the hill, which made for a perfect setting to speak to a large audience. Instead, Jesus comes down from the mount and walks among the people as he speaks. Jesus is among them, not as a figure towering over them, but as one who has compassion upon each and every person and walks side by side with them.

The second difference has to do with Luke's emphasis on Jesus' concern about the plight of the poor. Throughout the Gospel of Luke, those who suffer physical, mental, or psychological pain of any sort, those who grieve, those who are shunned, ignored, cast out, or condemned, are closest to his heart.

Hence, whereas in Matthew's Gospel Jesus says, "Blessed are the poor in spirit, for theirs is the kingdom of God," in Luke's Gospel, Jesus merely says, "Blessed are the poor, for they shall see God." It is not the "poor in spirit" but *ptokos*, an ancient Greek word meaning the "poorest of the poor." Theologians often speak of God's "preferential option for the poor," and Luke's portrait of Jesus reflects this. If you want to find Jesus, go look for him among the poor and the suffering and there you shall find him.

After Jesus' birth, his parents Joseph and Mary take Jesus to the temple, and Mary brings an offering of two turtledoves for the rite of purification. This was the offering acceptable for a poor family to make. Luke makes it known that Jesus was born into a poor family. No wonder when John's emissaries come to find out whether or not Jesus is the Messiah, Jesus tells them, "The poor have good news preached to them." Jesus could speak to the poor because he was one of them, and they were constantly in his heart. Luke's Gospel is known as the universal Gospel, because Luke's Jesus constantly breaks down the walls that divide people and builds bridges that bring people closer to God.

For Luke, Jesus' compassionate breadth and depth extend beyond the poor and suffering to those on the margins of society. Throughout Luke's Gospel and in the book of Acts, the ministry and role of women is highlighted. The birth narrative in Luke's Gospel is told from the perspective of Mary. Luke includes the experiences of women such as Mary's cousin Elizabeth, the prophet Anna, the widow of Nain, and the woman who anointed Jesus' feet with her hair. It is Luke who makes Mary Magdalene as well as Martha and Mary come alive and figure prominently in his story. And, Luke's Jesus makes a Samaritan a hero in the parable, even though Samaritans were much-despised by the Jews.

Luke was also a historian. He begins his gospel with four verses that scholars say are the best Greek found in the entire New Testament. Two chapters later, Luke anchors Jesus' ministry in time, writing in a most historical fashion, noting, "In the fifteenth year of the reign of Emperor Tiberius, when Pontius Pilate was governor of Judea, and Herod was ruler of Galilee, and his brother Philip ruler of the region of Ituraea and Trachonitis, and Lysanias ruler of Abilene, during the high priesthood of Annas and Caiaphas, the word of God came to John son of Zechariah in the wilderness." (3:1-2)

Among the evangelists, Luke was the only Gentile. He was clearly writing to share the life and ministry of Jesus with a Gentile audience. Hence, he translates Hebrew words into Greek or gives their Greek equivalent. Simon the Cananaean in Matthew appears as Simon the Zealot in Luke. Calvary is not called by its Hebrew name but is known as Golgatha, its Greek equivalent. Luke avoids the Jewish term "rabbi" and always has the disciples refer to Jesus as "master." When tracing Jesus' ancestry, he does not stop, like Matthew, at Abraham, the father of the Jewish race, but traces Jesus back to Adam.

A careful analysis of the Greek used in the Gospel of Luke and the book of Acts reveals that the same writer wrote both, employing a similar vocabulary and the same writing style. In addition, both books begin with an address to "most excellent Theophilus," who may have been a wealthy benefactor who commissioned Luke to write these works or a high official in the Roman government for whom Luke was attempting to tell the story of Jesus and the birth of the Church. The word "Theophilus" literally means "lover of God." Hence, the address "most excellent Theophilus" may actually refer to you and me, who seek to know, love, and serve God.

As a trusted companion of Paul, Luke met and spent time with the leaders of the early church. He witnessed the people of the Way, as the first Christians were known, come together to create the Church. He was imprisoned with Paul in Caesarea. Luke knew what it was like to suffer for the sake of the gospel. One can only imagine the conversations that Paul and Luke shared.

It is said that if Luke's Gospel were performed on stage, it would be a musical. Throughout, characters stop and break into song.

After receiving the news that she would bear the Son of God and usher Jesus into the world, Mary launches into song and gives us the *Magnificat*—the Church's most important song, which lifts up hope for the poor and warns the rich that the tables will be turned if they do not care for those in need. We also discover the *Nunc Dimittis*, sung by Simeon after he has beheld the baby Jesus and recognized him as God's Messiah, and Zechariah's *Benedictus*. In Luke, everyone has a song to sing.

Finally, prayer is prominent in Luke's Gospel. Often, as Jesus prepares to do something significant, he begins with prayer. Jesus prays at his baptism. Before selecting his disciples, Jesus prays. Before taking on the Pharisees, Jesus prays. Before Jesus asks his disciples who they think he is, he prays. Before predicting his death, Jesus spends time with God in prayer. At the Transfiguration, hanging on the cross, and before Peter denies him three times, Jesus prays. Jesus reveals prayer as our lifeline to God, as are the words of scripture.

In one of the final stories told in his Gospel, Luke alone offers the story of the encounter with Jesus on the road to Emmaus. Two disciples, lost in thought and buried in grief, are trying to comprehend what had gone so wrong in Jerusalem. They are just beginning to come to terms with Jesus' gruesome death, when they encounter a stranger, who sidles up to them as they walk. "What are you discussing?" he asks. "Are you the only stranger in Jerusalem who does not know the things that have taken place there?" they reply. Then Jesus opens up the scriptures and reveals everything that the Bible has to say about him, and the disciples' hearts burn like fire. So, too, as we read Luke's Gospel, our hearts burn like fire and Jesus comes alive among us so that we might live lives full of compassion, mercy, and love.

**The Rev. Marek P. Zabriskie**

*A Journey with Luke*

# A Journey
# with Luke

## *The 50 Day Bible Challenge*

## Luke 1:1-25

1 Since many have undertaken to set down an orderly account of the events that have been fulfilled among us, ²just as they were handed on to us by those who from the beginning were eyewitnesses and servants of the word, ³I too decided, after investigating everything carefully from the very first, to write an orderly account for you, most excellent Theophilus, ⁴so that you may know the truth concerning the things about which you have been instructed.

⁵In the days of King Herod of Judea, there was a priest named Zechariah, who belonged to the priestly order of Abijah. His wife was a descendant of Aaron, and her name was Elizabeth. ⁶Both of them were righteous before God, living blamelessly according to all the commandments and regulations of the Lord. ⁷But they had no children, because Elizabeth was barren, and both were getting on in years. ⁸Once when he was serving as priest before God and his section was on duty, ⁹he was chosen by lot, according to the custom of the priesthood, to enter the sanctuary of the Lord and offer incense. ¹⁰Now at the time of the incense offering, the whole assembly of the people was praying outside. ¹¹Then there appeared to him an angel of the Lord, standing at the right side of the altar of incense. ¹²When Zechariah saw him, he was terrified; and fear overwhelmed him. ¹³But the angel said to him, "Do not be afraid, Zechariah, for your prayer has been heard. Your wife Elizabeth will bear you a son, and you will name him John. ¹⁴You will have joy and gladness, and many will

rejoice at his birth, [15]for he will be great in the sight of the Lord. He must never drink wine or strong drink; even before his birth he will be filled with the Holy Spirit. [16]He will turn many of the people of Israel to the Lord their God. [17]With the spirit and power of Elijah he will go before him, to turn the hearts of parents to their children, and the disobedient to the wisdom of the righteous, to make ready a people prepared for the Lord." [18]Zechariah said to the angel, "How will I know that this is so? For I am an old man, and my wife is getting on in years." [19]The angel replied, "I am Gabriel. I stand in the presence of God, and I have been sent to speak to you and to bring you this good news. [20]But now, because you did not believe my words, which will be fulfilled in their time, you will become mute, unable to speak, until the day these things occur." [21]Meanwhile the people were waiting for Zechariah, and wondered at his delay in the sanctuary. [22]When he did come out, he could not speak to them, and they realized that he had seen a vision in the sanctuary. He kept motioning to them and remained unable to speak. [23]When his time of service was ended, he went to his home. [24]After those days his wife Elizabeth conceived, and for five months she remained in seclusion. She said, [25]"This is what the Lord has done for me when he looked favorably on me and took away the disgrace I have endured among my people."

# Reflection

How would you tell the story of Jesus? Luke begins his version using a traditional Hellenistic approach that invites the listener into the story, while at the same time highlights the research that has gone into his account. In this way, we are also invited into the telling and sharing of the gospel that has gone on since the time of Jesus.

Beginning not with Mary and Joseph, but with Elizabeth and Zechariah, Luke calls to mind the great exemplars of faith, Abraham and Sarah, reminding us that Jesus comes from a long line of faithful people.

Pouring it on thick now, Luke highlights Zechariah's use of incense, a privilege usually granted to priests only once in a lifetime. Zechariah's vision in the temple evokes Elijah, making the point that Jesus comes from the most faithful people of Israel. But his relatives are also human, as we can see when Zechariah doubts the promise of God.

Poor Zechariah must leave the temple, unable to speak, and confront all the people waiting expectantly. Imagine his challenge as he beholds the promise of God and also feels ashamed because of his faithlessness.

In this short beginning, Luke puts the listener on notice: no one is untouched when they draw near to God's blessings in the story of Jesus that will unfold. All will be transformed in unlikely ways.

**The Rev. William Lupfer**
**Rector of Trinity Wall Street**
**New York City, New York**

## Questions

Are you open to God's surprises like Elizabeth, or do you attempt to keep God squarely in a place that you can control and access, like Zechariah?

Are you ready to open your heart and live faithfully, come what may?

## Prayer

Oh God of unchangeable power and might. Draw near to us as we open our hearts to your awesome and bewildering blessings. Give birth to new faith in our hearts and guide us when we waver. We ask this in the name of Jesus. *Amen.*

## Luke 1:26–56

²⁶In the sixth month the angel Gabriel was sent by God to a town in Galilee called Nazareth, ²⁷to a virgin engaged to a man whose name was Joseph, of the house of David. The virgin's name was Mary. ²⁸And he came to her and said, "Greetings, favored one! The Lord is with you." ²⁹But she was much perplexed by his words and pondered what sort of greeting this might be. ³⁰The angel said to her, "Do not be afraid, Mary, for you have found favor with God. ³¹And now, you will conceive in your womb and bear a son, and you will name him Jesus. ³²He will be great, and will be called the Son of the Most High, and the Lord God will give to him the throne of his ancestor David. ³³He will reign over the house of Jacob forever, and of his kingdom there will be no end." ³⁴Mary said to the angel, "How can this be, since I am a virgin?" ³⁵The angel said to her, "The Holy Spirit will come upon you, and the power of the Most High will overshadow you; therefore the child to be born will be holy; he will be called Son of God. ³⁶And now, your relative Elizabeth in her old age has also conceived a son; and this is the sixth month for her who was said to be barren. ³⁷For nothing will be impossible with God." ³⁸Then Mary said, "Here am I, the servant of the Lord; let it be with me according to your word." Then the angel departed from her.

³⁹In those days Mary set out and went with haste to a Judean town in the hill country, ⁴⁰where she entered the house of Zechariah and greeted Elizabeth. ⁴¹When Elizabeth heard Mary's greeting, the child leaped in her womb.

And Elizabeth was filled with the Holy Spirit ⁴²and exclaimed with a loud cry, "Blessed are you among women, and blessed is the fruit of your womb. ⁴³And why has this happened to me, that the mother of my Lord comes to me? ⁴⁴For as soon as I heard the sound of your greeting, the child in my womb leaped for joy. ⁴⁵And blessed is she who believed that there would be a fulfillment of what was spoken to her by the Lord." ⁴⁶And Mary said, "My soul magnifies the Lord, ⁴⁷and my spirit rejoices in God my Savior, ⁴⁸for he has looked with favor on the lowliness of his servant. Surely, from now on all generations will call me blessed; ⁴⁹for the Mighty One has done great things for me, and holy is his name. ⁵⁰His mercy is for those who fear him from generation to generation. ⁵¹He has shown strength with his arm; he has scattered the proud in the thoughts of their hearts. ⁵²He has brought down the powerful from their thrones, and lifted up the lowly; ⁵³he has filled the hungry with good things, and sent the rich away empty. ⁵⁴He has helped his servant Israel, in remembrance of his mercy, ⁵⁵according to the promise he made to our ancestors, to Abraham and to his descendants forever." ⁵⁶And Mary remained with her about three months and then returned to her home.

# Reflection

In clear, crisp language, Luke announces the birth of Jesus in a similar manner as he did with John's birth. God sends the angel Gabriel to deliver the message, and he invokes the ancient houses and beloved historical figures of Israel: this time, David and Jacob.

The angel Gabriel has some work to do in order to convince Mary of the improbable events that will come to her. And she doesn't hesitate to ask questions. Gabriel talks about Elizabeth's pregnancy as a sign of God's power. Mary commends herself to God's power even though it puts her at grave risk as an unwed mother.

Now that they are both aligned with God's bewildering, transformative power, Mary and Elizabeth come together as two women who love each other and love the God who has surprised them. They both have been given huge, transformative gifts for which neither of them likely feel ready. Yet their joy in one another is palpable. Elizabeth's joyful acclamation is offered in a powerful, feminine, prophetic voice.

Mary's response is strong, powerful, and prophetic. She sings a song that confidently loops her own personal experience into the larger narrative of God's power and love—past, present, and future. Mary's words are at once historical and timeless, courageous and faithful. She is exactly the person the Son of God needs to help him grow into the full stature of humanity.

**The Rev. William Lupfer**
**Rector of Trinity Wall Street**
**New York City, New York**

## Questions_____

How has God surprised you with a challenge you thought was too much to bear?

Whom did you seek out to do the tough work of understanding the challenge as a blessing?

Was your response as faithful as Mary's and Elizabeth's?

## Prayer_____

Dear God of surprise and delight, give us strength when you bless us in ways that seem too challenging to bear. As you did for Mary and Elizabeth, give us mentors and guides who can help us find our way to you, even as you stay close to our hearts. We ask this in the name of Jesus. *Amen.*

## Luke 1:57-80

⁵⁷Now the time came for Elizabeth to give birth, and she bore a son. ⁵⁸Her neighbors and relatives heard that the Lord had shown his great mercy to her, and they rejoiced with her. ⁵⁹On the eighth day they came to circumcise the child, and they were going to name him Zechariah after his father. ⁶⁰But his mother said, "No; he is to be called John." ⁶¹They said to her, "None of your relatives has this name." ⁶²Then they began motioning to his father to find out what name he wanted to give him. ⁶³He asked for a writing tablet and wrote, "His name is John." And all of them were amazed. ⁶⁴Immediately his mouth was opened and his tongue freed, and he began to speak, praising God. ⁶⁵Fear came over all their neighbors, and all these things were talked about throughout the entire hill country of Judea. ⁶⁶All who heard them pondered them and said, "What then will this child become?" For, indeed, the hand of the Lord was with him.

⁶⁷Then his father Zechariah was filled with the Holy Spirit and spoke this prophecy: ⁶⁸"Blessed be the Lord God of Israel, for he has looked favorably on his people and redeemed them. ⁶⁹He has raised up a mighty savior for us in the house of his servant David, ⁷⁰as he spoke through the mouth of his holy prophets from of old, ⁷¹that we would be saved from our enemies and from the hand of all who hate us. ⁷²Thus he has shown the mercy promised to our ancestors, and has remembered his holy covenant, ⁷³the oath that he swore to our ancestor Abraham, to grant us ⁷⁴that we, being rescued from the hands of

our enemies, might serve him without fear, [75]in holiness and righteousness before him all our days. [76]And you, child, will be called the prophet of the Most High; for you will go before the Lord to prepare his ways, [77]to give knowledge of salvation to his people by the forgiveness of their sins. [78]By the tender mercy of our God, the dawn from on high will break upon us, [79]to give light to those who sit in darkness and in the shadow of death, to guide our feet into the way of peace." [80]The child grew and became strong in spirit, and he was in the wilderness until the day he appeared publicly to Israel.

# Reflection

Luke tells the story of John's birth and early years in three units: the birth, circumcision, and naming of John (1:57-66); the Benedictus (1:67-79); and a summary statement (1:80). The three units have parallels with three units in the story of Jesus: the birth, circumcision, and naming (2:1-21), the Magnificat (1:46-55), and a summary (2:52). The parallels emphasize both the similarities and the differences between the two.

The focus of the story of John's birth is on the naming of John. The only evidence that we have for naming a child at the time of circumcision comes several centuries later. The Roman historian Josephus tells us that male children were often named after their grandfather (Life 1.5) and sometimes their father (The Jewish War 5.534), as our story presupposes. However, first Elizabeth and then Zechariah object and insist on keeping the instructions that Gabriel had given Zechariah in the temple by naming the child John. After Zechariah wrote his request, he regained his speech: the doubt that he had originally expressed had become faith. The story of John's birth is a story about the faith of his parents.

It was the faith of Zechariah that led him to break into a burst of praise. We know the song by the name of the first word in the Latin translation: Benedictus. The hymn in Luke consists of two parts: a prayer of thanksgiving (1:68-75) and a prayer for the newborn, a genethliakon (1:76-79). The hymn is a joyous expression of the faith that God works in human history. The summary reminds us that this messenger of God was a developing human.

**Gregory E. Sterling**
**Dean of the Yale Divinity School**
**New Haven, Connecticut**

## Questions

These texts deliberately create a Jewish environment. How important is it for us to understand that the story of Jesus is anchored in Judaism?

What does this tell us about Jewish-Christian relations?

## Prayer

God, thank you for the ways that you work among human beings. Help parents to come to the joyous and optimistic faith of Elizabeth and Zechariah. May the children whom we raise serve as lights in a world of darkness. Free our tongues to sing your praise. *Amen.*

## Luke 2:1-21

2 In those days a decree went out from Emperor Augustus that all the world should be registered. [2]This was the first registration and was taken while Quirinius was governor of Syria. [3]All went to their own towns to be registered. [4]Joseph also went from the town of Nazareth in Galilee to Judea, to the city of David called Bethlehem, because he was descended from the house and family of David. [5]He went to be registered with Mary, to whom he was engaged and who was expecting a child. [6]While they were there, the time came for her to deliver her child. [7]And she gave birth to her firstborn son and wrapped him in bands of cloth, and laid him in a manger, because there was no place for them in the inn.

[8]In that region there were shepherds living in the fields, keeping watch over their flock by night. [9]Then an angel of the Lord stood before them, and the glory of the Lord shone around them, and they were terrified. [10]But the angel said to them, "Do not be afraid; for see—I am bringing you good news of great joy for all the people: [11]to you is born this day in the city of David a Savior, who is the Messiah, the Lord. [12]This will be a sign for you: you will find a child wrapped in bands of cloth and lying in a manger." [13]And suddenly there was with the angel a multitude of the heavenly host, praising God and saying, [14]"Glory to God in the highest heaven, and on earth peace among those whom he favors!" [15]When the angels had left them and gone into heaven, the shepherds said to one another, "Let us go now to Bethlehem and see this thing

that has taken place, which the Lord has made known to us." <sup>16</sup>So they went with haste and found Mary and Joseph, and the child lying in the manger. <sup>17</sup>When they saw this, they made known what had been told them about this child; <sup>18</sup>and all who heard it were amazed at what the shepherds told them. <sup>19</sup>But Mary treasured all these words and pondered them in her heart. <sup>20</sup>The shepherds returned, glorifying and praising God for all they had heard and seen, as it had been told them.

<sup>21</sup>After eight days had passed, it was time to circumcise the child; and he was called Jesus, the name given by the angel before he was conceived in the womb.

# Reflection

The story of Jesus' birth falls into three units: the census and the birth, the reaction of the shepherds, and the circumcision and naming of Jesus. There are no references to John; the focus is on Jesus.

Luke situates the story of Jesus' birth against the backdrop of the Roman Empire. This places Christianity on the world stage: Christianity can be understood not as a hermetically sealed movement but as a movement in the larger world. The reference to Augustus invites a comparison between the emperor and the newborn: the Pax Augustana is contrasted with the "peace among those whom he favors." The census moves Joseph and Mary from Nazareth to Bethlehem, the city of David. It is here that Jesus is born in humble circumstances.

Luke chooses not to provide details about Jesus' birth but to relate the reaction to it. We do not see Jesus through the eyes of Roman senators or even provincial officials but through the eyes of shepherds! The evangelist tells the story of the birth announcement using a standard form found in birth announcements in the Old Testament: the appearance of an angel, a reaction of fear, a divine message, and a sign. The outburst of a heavenly chorus invites us as readers to join in the song. The visit of the shepherds is an anticlimax, but it challenges us to think about the significance of the birth. The note about circumcision and naming reminds us that Jesus was a Jew.

**Gregory E. Sterling**
**Dean of the Yale Divinity School**
**New Haven, Connecticut**

## Questions

How important is it that Luke omits the details about Jesus' birth and focuses on the setting in the Roman world and the reaction of the shepherds?

Does it help us to think about the significance of Jesus for the larger world and the need to see that significance through the eyes of the lowly?

## Prayer

God, help us to understand the responsibilities that we have as Christians in the larger world. May we find the wisdom both to negotiate our place within the world and to transform it. May we always remember that we do so by looking from the bottom up rather than the top down. *Amen.*

## Luke 2:22-52

²²When the time came for their purification according to the law of Moses, they brought him up to Jerusalem to present him to the Lord ²³(as it is written in the law of the Lord, "Every firstborn male shall be designated as holy to the Lord"), ²⁴and they offered a sacrifice according to what is stated in the law of the Lord, "a pair of turtledoves or two young pigeons."

²⁵Now there was a man in Jerusalem whose name was Simeon; this man was righteous and devout, looking forward to the consolation of Israel, and the Holy Spirit rested on him. ²⁶It had been revealed to him by the Holy Spirit that he would not see death before he had seen the Lord's Messiah. ²⁷Guided by the Spirit, Simeon came into the temple; and when the parents brought in the child Jesus, to do for him what was customary under the law, ²⁸Simeon took him in his arms and praised God, saying, ²⁹"Master, now you are dismissing your servant in peace, according to your word; ³⁰for my eyes have seen your salvation, ³¹which you have prepared in the presence of all peoples, ³²a light for revelation to the Gentiles and for glory to your people Israel." ³³And the child's father and mother were amazed at what was being said about him. ³⁴Then Simeon blessed them and said to his mother Mary, "This child is destined for the falling and the rising of many in Israel, and to be a sign that will be opposed ³⁵so that the inner thoughts of many will be revealed—and a sword will pierce your own soul too." ³⁶There was also a prophet, Anna the daughter of Phanuel, of the tribe of Asher. She was of a great age, having

lived with her husband seven years after her marriage, <sup>37</sup>then as a widow to the age of eighty-four. She never left the temple but worshiped there with fasting and prayer night and day. <sup>38</sup>At that moment she came, and began to praise God and to speak about the child to all who were looking for the redemption of Jerusalem. <sup>39</sup>When they had finished everything required by the law of the Lord, they returned to Galilee, to their own town of Nazareth. <sup>40</sup>The child grew and became strong, filled with wisdom; and the favor of God was upon him.

<sup>41</sup>Now every year his parents went to Jerusalem for the festival of the Passover. <sup>42</sup>And when he was twelve years old, they went up as usual for the festival. <sup>43</sup>When the festival was ended and they started to return, the boy Jesus stayed behind in Jerusalem, but his parents did not know it. <sup>44</sup>Assuming that he was in the group of travelers, they went a day's journey. Then they started to look for him among their relatives and friends. <sup>45</sup>When they did not find him, they returned to Jerusalem to search for him. <sup>46</sup>After three days they found him in the temple, sitting among the teachers, listening to them and asking them questions. <sup>47</sup>And all who heard him were amazed at his understanding and his answers. <sup>48</sup>When his parents saw him they were astonished; and his mother said to him, "Child, why have you treated us like this? Look, your father and I have been searching for you in great anxiety." <sup>49</sup>He said to them, "Why were you searching for me? Did you not know that I must be in my Father's house?" <sup>50</sup>But they did not understand what he said to them. <sup>51</sup>Then he went down with them and came to Nazareth, and was obedient to them. His mother treasured all these things in her heart. <sup>52</sup>And Jesus increased in wisdom and in years, and in divine and human favor.

# Reflection

Mary and Joseph carried the infant Jesus in their arms and offered him in the temple according to the tradition of their elders. They did this act as it had been done for centuries, respecting the customs of their faith community.

This image is important for us. None of us come to faith except by being carried. Many of us, like Jesus, were literally carried to the temple of the New Covenant and to the font, the womb of our rebirth as children of the Risen One. Others of us found our way to the font of new life perhaps without literally being carried but transported no less on the prayers, urgings, and invitations of those who loved us.

To be carried, one must let go; one must yield; one must trust; one must relax oneself into the strength of another. We've all experienced picking up a child when he or she does not want to be carried. Many of us know something about carrying an aging adult. That, too, can be nearly impossible unless our elder finds safety and comfort in being cradled and carried.

Remember those who have carried you to Jesus: a parent, a friend, someone who loves you dearly. Perhaps you sense that you've been carried on the prayers of saints and angels or by persons whose names you do not even know. Pray for those who carried you and stretch your arms to carry another.

**The Rt. Rev. J. Neil Alexander**
**Dean of the School of Theology of the University of the South**
**Sewanee, Tennessee**

## Question

When you reflect upon being carried to Jesus, what wells up within you as you consider your call to carry others?

## Prayer

Holy and gracious God: we give you thanks for the faithfulness of Mary and Joseph in carrying Jesus to the temple. We praise you also for Blessed Simeon and Holy Anna whose arms welcomed and received him. Make us mindful of those who carried us to the font and give us glad hearts and open arms to receive those you send our way. All this we ask in Jesus' name. *Amen.*

## Luke 3:1-20

3 In the fifteenth year of the reign of Emperor Tiberius, when Pontius Pilate was governor of Judea, and Herod was ruler of Galilee, and his brother Philip ruler of the region of Ituraea and Trachonitis, and Lysanias ruler of Abilene, ²during the high priesthood of Annas and Caiaphas, the word of God came to John son of Zechariah in the wilderness. ³He went into all the region around the Jordan, proclaiming a baptism of repentance for the forgiveness of sins, ⁴as it is written in the book of the words of the prophet Isaiah, "The voice of one crying out in the wilderness: 'Prepare the way of the Lord, make his paths straight. ⁵Every valley shall be filled, and every mountain and hill shall be made low, and the crooked shall be made straight, and the rough ways made smooth; ⁶and all flesh shall see the salvation of God.'" ⁷John said to the crowds that came out to be baptized by him, "You brood of vipers! Who warned you to flee from the wrath to come? ⁸Bear fruits worthy of repentance. Do not begin to say to yourselves, 'We have Abraham as our ancestor'; for I tell you, God is able from these stones to raise up children to Abraham. ⁹Even now the ax is lying at the root of the trees; every tree therefore that does not bear good fruit is cut down and thrown into the fire." ¹⁰And the crowds asked him, "What then should we do?" ¹¹In reply he said to them, "Whoever has two coats must share with anyone who has none; and whoever has food must do likewise." ¹²Even tax collectors came to be baptized, and they asked him, "Teacher, what should we do?" ¹³He said to them, "Collect no more than

the amount prescribed for you." [14]Soldiers also asked him, "And we, what should we do?" He said to them, "Do not extort money from anyone by threats or false accusation, and be satisfied with your wages."

[15]As the people were filled with expectation, and all were questioning in their hearts concerning John, whether he might be the Messiah, [16]John answered all of them by saying, "I baptize you with water; but one who is more powerful than I is coming; I am not worthy to untie the thong of his sandals. He will baptize you with the Holy Spirit and fire. [17]His winnowing fork is in his hand, to clear his threshing floor and to gather the wheat into his granary; but the chaff he will burn with unquenchable fire." [18]So, with many other exhortations, he proclaimed the good news to the people. [19]But Herod the ruler, who had been rebuked by him because of Herodias, his brother's wife, and because of all the evil things that Herod had done, [20]added to them all by shutting up John in prison.

# Reflection

The intensity of our joy and delight is most often the result of the depth of our expectation and anticipation. Knowing something good is coming, something exciting, something desirable, but not knowing exactly what or when or where, stimulates our interest and invites us to look forward with renewed energy. The thrill and elation of the coming discovery fills us to overflowing. Can you imagine a rich, full, and joyful life apart from liberal amounts of expectation and anticipation?

So much of the Gospel of Luke is cast against a background of hope and expectation. God is not finished; there is more to come; we have seen in part, there is more to come. John the Baptist bears witness; there is more to come! There's a new age breaking in: a new moment, a new day, a new world is coming. And our anticipation of this new age—living into the promise of it—is one of our deepest joys and one of God's most profound gifts.

John says get ready. Examine your life, bear fruit, share what you have, be faithful, be honest, and do what is right. Why? Because the one who is coming is going to turn everything upside down. The one who is coming imagines a different kind of world, unbound, unlimited by our self-made restraints, and open wide to God and what God desires to do among us. The anticipation of God's promises—and the Promised One—thrills our hearts and delights our souls.

**The Rt. Rev. J. Neil Alexander**
**Dean of the School of Theology of the University of the South**
**Sewanee, Tennessee**

## Question

From what do you need to be unbound so that your expectation and anticipation of what God wants to do in your life can soar?

## Prayer

Holy God: we give you thanks for the gifts of hope and expectation. Instill in us, we pray, a lively sense of anticipation and joy, that our hearts may long for your presence in our lives and look with eagerness for the new world that you continue to unfold before us. All this we ask in the name of Jesus. *Amen.*

## Luke 3:21-38

21Now when all the people were baptized, and when Jesus also had been baptized and was praying, the heaven was opened, 22and the Holy Spirit descended upon him in bodily form like a dove. And a voice came from heaven, "You are my Son, the Beloved; with you I am well pleased." 23Jesus was about thirty years old when he began his work. He was the son (as was thought) of Joseph son of Heli, 24son of Matthat, son of Levi, son of Melchi, son of Jannai, son of Joseph, 25son of Mattathias, son of Amos, son of Nahum, son of Esli, son of Naggai, 26son of Maath, son of Mattathias, son of Semein, son of Josech, son of Joda, 27son of Joanan, son of Rhesa, son of Zerubbabel, son of Shealtiel, son of Neri, 28son of Melchi, son of Addi, son of Cosam, son of Elmadam, son of Er, 29son of Joshua, son of Eliezer, son of Jorim, son of Matthat, son of Levi, 30son of Simeon, son of Judah, son of Joseph, son of Jonam, son of Eliakim, 31son of Melea, son of Menna, son of Mattatha, son of Nathan, son of David, 32son of Jesse, son of Obed, son of Boaz, son of Sala, son of Nahshon, 33son of Amminadab, son of Admin, son of Arni, son of Hezron, son of Perez, son of Judah, 34son of Jacob, son of Isaac, son of Abraham, son of Terah, son of Nahor, 35son of Serug, son of Reu, son of Peleg, son of Eber, son of Shelah, 36son of Cainan, son of Arphaxad, son of Shem, son of Noah, son of Lamech, 37son of Methuselah, son of Enoch, son of Jared, son of Mahalaleel, son of Cainan, 38son of Enos, son of Seth, son of Adam, son of God.

# Reflection

How deceptive artistic depictions of Jesus' baptism often are—when they portray him in splendid isolation. Luke reminds us that John's baptisms were crowd scenes. Jesus is one of the masses seeking that purifying new beginning in anticipation of the onset of God's reign. As if to remind us of Jesus' solidarity with ordinary people in their confusion and struggle, Luke goes on to give us Jesus' genealogy traced through Joseph all the way back to Adam, the ancestor of all humankind. Jesus' uniqueness is not one that sets him apart. Paradoxically, he is uniquely "the Son of Man," the one called by God to reconnect us as human beings to one another by our rewoven intimacy with the Creator—the new Adam, as Paul would say.

Luke is writing primarily for those who know that Jesus' experience of the descent of the Spirit, and the thrilling words of the heavenly Father, "You are my Son, the Beloved; with you I am well pleased," were not for him alone. Through our baptism into Christ, we receive the same Spirit and are adopted as beloved children. We are not meant to read this passage as if it were about a unique experience, exclusive to Jesus. We are jolted into awareness of our union with Christ, our shared experience in and with him. Verse 23 mentions "when he began his work," so we recall that he has given us a share in this work as members of his body.

**The Rev. Martin L. Smith**
**Author and retreat leader**
**Washington, DC**

## Questions

Do you accept the words "in you I am well pleased" as truly addressed to you because you are a member of Christ's body?

If you find it difficult, are you prepared to ask for that experience now in prayer?

## Prayer

Jesus, you have made me a fellow worker with you in God's work of healing. Today I bring to mind my baptism so that I can take up this work again as a beloved child of God endowed with the same Spirit that empowered you. Help me remember who I really am. *Amen.*

## Luke 4:1-13

Jesus, full of the Holy Spirit, returned from the Jordan and was led by the Spirit in the wilderness, ²where for forty days he was tempted by the devil. He ate nothing at all during those days, and when they were over, he was famished. ³The devil said to him, "If you are the Son of God, command this stone to become a loaf of bread." ⁴Jesus answered him, "It is written, 'One does not live by bread alone.'" ⁵Then the devil led him up and showed him in an instant all the kingdoms of the world. ⁶And the devil said to him, "To you I will give their glory and all this authority; for it has been given over to me, and I give it to anyone I please. ⁷If you, then, will worship me, it will all be yours." ⁸Jesus answered him, "It is written, 'Worship the Lord your God, and serve only him.'" ⁹Then the devil took him to Jerusalem, and placed him on the pinnacle of the temple, saying to him, "If you are the Son of God, throw yourself down from here, ¹⁰for it is written, 'He will command his angels concerning you, to protect you,' ¹¹and 'On their hands they will bear you up, so that you will not dash your foot against a stone.'" ¹²Jesus answered him, "It is said, 'Do not put the Lord your God to the test.'" ¹³When the devil had finished every test, he departed from him until an opportune time.

# Reflection

We can be sure that the plea to God, "Save us from the time of trial," which Jesus taught his disciples to pray, is something that Jesus had to keep on praying himself. It is a prayer that our Father will spare us the stress of an ordeal in which we might fall away from our dependence on him and be proved unworthy. Today's story of Jesus' trial in the wilderness soon after his baptism gives us a clue to the urgency of the prayer he taught us.

Like an engineer whose role is to subject a device to a stress test to see what may break it, the devil presents Jesus with shortcuts to success that bypass the appalling vulnerability of God's path of nonviolent love: the shortcut of magic and miracle, the shortcut of authoritarian power, the shortcut of privilege that disdains to submit to the norms under which ordinary people must live and suffer. In each case Jesus renews his commitment to the path of suffering love in naked dependence on God.

Luke is the evangelist who reminds us that this test was only the first of many. "When the devil had finished every test, he departed from him until an opportune time." He will be back—in the ordeal of Gethsemane and in the final struggle to deter Jesus from surrendering himself entirely to the cross for our sake. But Jesus did not "come down from the cross!"

**The Rev. Martin L. Smith**
**Author and retreat leader**
**Washington, DC**

## Questions

Do you recognize stresses in your life that make you want to use rather than serve others?

Have you pictured recently the kind of real-life trials that you fear might tempt you to turn your back on God—and prayed to God to spare you from them?

## Prayer

Loving God, when I pray the Lord's Prayer how seldom I pause to think of "the time of trial" from which I am asking to be spared! Help me to accept my vulnerability to losing my faith in a crisis or cruel hardship. May your Spirit, the inner Encourager you have given us, protect me always and help me endure whatever ordeals I must undergo on life's journey. In Jesus' name I pray. *Amen.*

## Luke 4:14-44

¹⁴Then Jesus, filled with the power of the Spirit, returned to Galilee, and a report about him spread through all the surrounding country. ¹⁵He began to teach in their synagogues and was praised by everyone. ¹⁶When he came to Nazareth, where he had been brought up, he went to the synagogue on the sabbath day, as was his custom. He stood up to read, ¹⁷and the scroll of the prophet Isaiah was given to him. He unrolled the scroll and found the place where it was written: ¹⁸"The Spirit of the Lord is upon me, because he has anointed me to bring good news to the poor. He has sent me to proclaim release to the captives and recovery of sight to the blind, to let the oppressed go free, ¹⁹to proclaim the year of the Lord's favor." ²⁰And he rolled up the scroll, gave it back to the attendant, and sat down.

The eyes of all in the synagogue were fixed on him. ²¹Then he began to say to them, "Today this scripture has been fulfilled in your hearing." ²²All spoke well of him and were amazed at the gracious words that came from his mouth. They said, "Is not this Joseph's son?" ²³He said to them, "Doubtless you will quote to me this proverb, 'Doctor, cure yourself!' And you will say, 'Do here also in your hometown the things that we have heard you did at Capernaum.'" ²⁴And he said, "Truly I tell you, no prophet is accepted in the prophet's hometown. ²⁵But the truth is, there were many widows in Israel in the time of Elijah, when the heaven was shut up three years and six months, and there was a severe famine over all the land; ²⁶yet Elijah was sent to none of them except to a widow at Zarephath in Sidon. ²⁷There were also many lepers in Israel in the time of the prophet Elisha, and none of them was cleansed except Naaman the Syrian." ²⁸When they heard this, all in the synagogue were filled with rage. ²⁹They got up, drove him out of the town, and led him to the brow of the hill on which their town was built, so that they might hurl him off the cliff. ³⁰But he passed through the midst of them and went on his way.

³¹He went down to Capernaum, a city in Galilee, and was teaching them on the sabbath. ³²They were astounded at his teaching, because he spoke with authority. ³³In the synagogue there was a man who had the spirit of an unclean demon, and he cried out with a loud voice, ³⁴"Let us alone! What have you to do with us, Jesus of Nazareth? Have you come to destroy us? I know who you are, the Holy One of God." ³⁵But Jesus rebuked him, saying, "Be silent, and come out of him!" When the demon had thrown him down before them, he came out of him without having done him any harm. ³⁶They were all amazed and kept saying to one another, "What kind of utterance is this? For with authority and power he commands the unclean spirits, and out they come!" ³⁷And a report about him began to reach every place in the region. ³⁸After leaving the synagogue he entered Simon's house. Now Simon's mother-in-law was suffering from a high fever, and they asked him about her. ³⁹Then he stood over her and rebuked the fever, and it left her. Immediately she got up and began to serve them. ⁴⁰As the sun was setting, all those who had any who were sick with various kinds of diseases brought them to him; and he laid his hands on each of them and cured them. ⁴¹Demons also came out of many, shouting, "You are the Son of God!" But he rebuked them and would not allow them

to speak, because they knew that he was the Messiah. ⁴²At daybreak he departed and went into a deserted place. And the crowds were looking for him; and when they reached him, they wanted to prevent him from leaving them. ⁴³But he said to them, "I must proclaim the good news of the kingdom of God to the other cities also; for I was sent for this purpose." ⁴⁴So he continued proclaiming the message in the synagogues of Judea.

# Reflection

The time of preparation for the ministry that lies ahead is over. Jesus returns to Nazareth where he grew up. His reputation as a miracle worker has gone before him, and he's welcomed back as the "local boy made good," even having the honor of being invited to take part in the synagogue service. He's handed the scroll of the prophet Isaiah and, as was the custom, can choose what he reads. And what a passage he chooses! It's the clue to how Jesus understood his ministry. It's about bringing good news to the poor, proclaiming release to captives, recovering sight to the blind, freeing the oppressed, and proclaiming the year of the Lord's favor. It's not a churchy ministry but an outward-facing ministry, serving those in need. It's the same ministry Jesus entrusts to us, to everyone who follows him. It's the pattern for our discipleship.

The crowd doesn't get it. Their welcome and praise turn quickly to anger and mob violence, foreshadowing the events of Palm Sunday and Good Friday. They want a miracle worker, but Jesus tells them that Elijah and Elisha worked miracles for those outside Israel. His ministry is for all people, a universal ministry.

Jesus continues his ministry, not from his hometown now but from Capernaum, healing the sick and casting out demons who recognize him as the Messiah and understand the threat his goodness is to them.

**Dame Mary Tanner**
**Ecumenist**
**Cambridge, England**

## Question

What does Jesus' understanding of his ministry mean for your ministry and for that of the community to which you belong?

## Prayer

Lord, grant us wisdom to understand the pattern of your ministry and the gift of your Holy Spirit. Empower us to follow that way in serving the poor and those in need. In Jesus' name we pray. *Amen.*

## Luke 5:1-16

5 Once while Jesus was standing beside the lake of Gennesaret, and the crowd was pressing in on him to hear the word of God, ²he saw two boats there at the shore of the lake; the fishermen had gone out of them and were washing their nets. ³He got into one of the boats, the one belonging to Simon, and asked him to put out a little way from the shore. Then he sat down and taught the crowds from the boat. ⁴When he had finished speaking, he said to Simon, "Put out into the deep water and let down your nets for a catch." ⁵Simon answered, "Master, we have worked all night long but have caught nothing. Yet if you say so, I will let down the nets." ⁶When they had done this, they caught so many fish that their nets were beginning to break. ⁷So they signaled their partners in the other boat to come and help them. And they came and filled both boats, so that they began to sink. ⁸But when Simon Peter saw it, he fell down at Jesus' knees, saying, "Go away from me, Lord, for I am a sinful man!" ⁹For he and all who were with him were amazed at the catch of fish that they had taken; ¹⁰and so also were James and John, sons of Zebedee, who were partners with Simon. Then Jesus said to Simon, "Do not be afraid; from now on you will be catching people." ¹¹When they had brought their boats to shore, they left everything and followed him.

¹²Once, when he was in one of the cities, there was a man covered with leprosy. When he saw Jesus, he bowed with his face to the ground and begged him, "Lord, if you choose, you can make me clean." ¹³Then

Jesus stretched out his hand, touched him, and said, "I do choose. Be made clean." Immediately the leprosy left him. [14]And he ordered him to tell no one. "Go," he said, "and show yourself to the priest, and, as Moses commanded, make an offering for your cleansing, for a testimony to them." [15]But now more than ever the word about Jesus spread abroad; many crowds would gather to hear him and to be cured of their diseases. [16]But he would withdraw to deserted places and pray.

# Reflection

Imagine early morning by the Sea of Galilee. Two boats are drawn up on the shore. Exhausted fishermen are washing their nets. A large crowd is gathering around a man, Jesus, pushing closer in their eagerness to hear him. He gets into Peter's boat and teaches the crowd. Then he tells Peter to cast the nets into the sea. Peter explains to him that it's pointless. They have fished all night and caught nothing. But they do cast the net again. Peter has recognized in Jesus an authority he must obey. The net is filled with so many fish that James and John take some of the catch into their boat. There's something bigger going on here, and Peter is not sure he can cope. He tells Jesus to go away, sensing in the presence of Jesus his own sinfulness. But Jesus replies reassuringly: "Do not be afraid; from now on you will be catching people." The catch of fish is an acted parable of the mission that lies ahead for the disciples. These fishermen have no idea where this will lead but they do leave everything and follow Jesus. As you read on in the gospel story, you will hear the call to follow coming again and again: to the disciples, to the crowds, to the people Jesus heals—and it comes to us.

Jesus' teaching and miracles, like the healing of the leper, attract large crowds. He has to get away from the sensation hunters, and he withdraws for a time of prayer. Times of solitude, waiting on his Father, are important times for reflecting on his ministry and for preparing himself for what lies ahead.

**Dame Mary Tanner**
**Ecumenist**
**Cambridge, England**

## Questions

When have you heard Jesus calling you, "Follow me"? What has been your response?

Are times of prayer, times of just being with God, a source of strength in your life?

## Prayer

Jesus, who called the disciples beside the Galilean Sea, may we, like them, follow you wherever you desire to lead us. May we, following your example, find time in our over-busy lives for prayer, time to understand what you would have us do to spread the good news of your kingdom in a hurting and violent world. *Amen.*

## Luke 5:17-39

¹⁷One day, while he was teaching, Pharisees and teachers of the law were sitting near by (they had come from every village of Galilee and Judea and from Jerusalem); and the power of the Lord was with him to heal. ¹⁸Just then some men came, carrying a paralyzed man on a bed. They were trying to bring him in and lay him before Jesus; ¹⁹but finding no way to bring him in because of the crowd, they went up on the roof and let him down with his bed through the tiles into the middle of the crowd in front of Jesus. ²⁰When he saw their faith, he said, "Friend, your sins are forgiven you." ²¹Then the scribes and the Pharisees began to question, "Who is this who is speaking blasphemies? Who can forgive sins but God alone?" ²²When Jesus perceived their questionings, he answered them, "Why do you raise such questions in your hearts? ²³Which is easier, to say, 'Your sins are forgiven you,' or to say, 'Stand up and walk'? ²⁴But so that you may know that the Son of Man has authority on earth to forgive sins" —he said to the one who was paralyzed— "I say to you, stand up and take your bed and go to your home." ²⁵Immediately he stood up before them, took what he had been lying on, and went to his home, glorifying God. ²⁶Amazement seized all of them, and they glorified God and were filled with awe, saying, "We have seen strange things today."

²⁷After this he went out and saw a tax collector named Levi, sitting at the tax booth; and he said to him, "Follow me." ²⁸And he got up, left everything, and followed him. ²⁹Then Levi

gave a great banquet for him in his house; and there was a large crowd of tax collectors and others sitting at the table with them. ³⁰The Pharisees and their scribes were complaining to his disciples, saying, "Why do you eat and drink with tax collectors and sinners?" ³¹Jesus answered, "Those who are well have no need of a physician, but those who are sick; ³²I have come to call not the righteous but sinners to repentance." ³³Then they said to him, "John's disciples, like the disciples of the Pharisees, frequently fast and pray, but your disciples eat and drink. ³⁴Jesus said to them, "You cannot make wedding guests fast while the bridegroom is with them, can you? ³⁵The days will come when the bridegroom will be taken away from them, and then they will fast in those days." ³⁶He also told them a parable: "No one tears a piece from a new garment and sews it on an old garment; otherwise the new will be torn, and the piece from the new will not match the old. ³⁷And no one puts new wine into old wineskins; otherwise the new wine will burst the skins and will be spilled, and the skins will be destroyed. ³⁸But new wine must be put into fresh wineskins. ³⁹And no one after drinking old wine desires new wine, but says, 'The old is good.'"

# Reflection

Think of the drama! A man is stricken. He cannot walk, work, or use the toilet. "Jesus could heal me," the man exclaims, "and he's in town!" Friends take up the man's stretcher and carry him to Jesus. But they are thwarted. The crowd around Jesus is too thick. The paralytic cries, "Just let me touch him!" They take the patient to the roof and airlift him to Jesus.

What does Jesus do? He sees their faith and then forgives the man's sins.

Healing, or even better, preventing paralysis is easy. We prevent paralysis every day with the polio vaccine. Forgiving sin is a different matter. There is only one person who has ever walked the earth and claimed the right to forgive sins: Jesus.

Jesus used his miracles not to show that he could restore sight or limbs but to establish that he had the right and the ability to forgive our sins.

Sin is not a popular topic today, and so we try to debunk its existence. First, we trivialize sin: "This chocolate is sinfully good!" "Those deviled eggs are to die for!" Second, we deny that sin exists: "Were those really Ten Commandments, or merely suggestions?" "I'm not sure God got it right in that verse about _____."

In trivializing sin, we deny Christ. We can be healed only by acknowledging our sins and believing that Christ can forgive them. It is through such faith that we can get up and walk into the light.

**Matthew Sleeth, MD**
**Executive Director of Blessed Earth**
**Lexington, Kentucky**

## Questions

Has sin become something you trivialize or deny?

Why do many healed by Jesus go about their business, but the paralytic praises God?

Why does Jesus say that those who are forgiven of greater debts (sins) have more reason to be grateful?

## Prayer

Lord, teach us to fear you so that we may gain wisdom. Help us to understand our sins so that we may acknowledge your forgiveness. Forgive us so that we may learn to forgive others and so that we may dwell with you in peace and joy forever. *Amen.*

## Luke 6:1-26

6One sabbath while Jesus was going through the grainfields, his disciples plucked some heads of grain, rubbed them in their hands, and ate them. ²But some of the Pharisees said, "Why are you doing what is not lawful on the sabbath?" ³Jesus answered, "Have you not read what David did when he and his companions were hungry? ⁴He entered the house of God and took and ate the bread of the Presence, which it is not lawful for any but the priests to eat, and gave some to his companions?" ⁵Then he said to them, "The Son of Man is lord of the sabbath." ⁶On another sabbath he entered the synagogue and taught, and there was a man there whose right hand was withered. ⁷The scribes and the Pharisees watched him to see whether he would cure on the sabbath, so that they might find an accusation against him. ⁸Even though he knew what they were thinking, he said to the man who had the withered hand, "Come and stand here." He got up and stood there. ⁹Then Jesus said to them, "I ask you, is it lawful to do good or to do harm on the sabbath, to save life or to destroy it?" ¹⁰After looking around at all of them, he said to him, "Stretch out your hand." He did so, and his hand was restored. ¹¹But they were filled with fury and discussed with one another what they might do to Jesus.

¹²Now during those days he went out to the mountain to pray; and he spent the night in prayer to God. ¹³And when day came, he called his disciples and chose twelve of them, whom he also named apostles: ¹⁴Simon, whom he named Peter, and his

brother Andrew, and James, and John, and Philip, and Bartholomew, ¹⁵and Matthew, and Thomas, and James son of Alphaeus, and Simon, who was called the Zealot, ¹⁶and Judas son of James, and Judas Iscariot, who became a traitor. ¹⁷He came down with them and stood on a level place, with a great crowd of his disciples and a great multitude of people from all Judea, Jerusalem, and the coast of Tyre and Sidon. ¹⁸They had come to hear him and to be healed of their diseases; and those who were troubled with unclean spirits were cured. ¹⁹And all in the crowd were trying to touch him, for power came out from him and healed all of them.

²⁰Then he looked up at his disciples and said: "Blessed are you who are poor, for yours is the kingdom of God. ²¹"Blessed are you who are hungry now, for you will be filled. "Blessed are you who weep now, for you will laugh. ²²"Blessed are you when people hate you, and when they exclude you, revile you, and defame you on account of the Son of Man. ²³Rejoice in that day and leap for joy, for surely your reward is great in heaven; for that is what their ancestors did to the prophets. ²⁴"But woe to you who are rich, for you have received your consolation. ²⁵"Woe to you who are full now, for you will be hungry. "Woe to you who are laughing now, for you will mourn and weep. ²⁶"Woe to you when all speak well of you, for that is what their ancestors did to the false prophets.

# Reflection

Jesus was a man of sorrows, but he was also a man of miracles. First of all, he was nearly impossible to kill. Since birth, people had tried to stone him and throw him off a cliff. But he could walk on water, stick ears back on, and feed five thousand out of a single lunch box.

On the sabbath, however, Jesus only performed one kind of miracle: he healed people. In today's reading, he proclaims himself lord of the sabbath. The Hebrew people of Jesus' time observed the sabbath, but they had forgotten the intent of the day. The intent wasn't to burden or enslave Israel but to free it and give it joy.

When Adam and Eve took a bite out of the apple, they lost a proper balance between work and rest. Jesus came to restore that balance. He came to give rest to the weary. For the last two thousand years, Christians have observed the sabbath. Ours is the first generation to work 24/7. Ironically, we do not have a pharaoh saying, "More bricks."

Today, many of us are chained to work by our phones. This Sunday, meditate upon a God who heals us through sabbath rest. Then push the button on the top of your phone for three seconds and break the chains. When you turn the phone back on, don't be surprised if the symbol of the fall appears—an apple with a missing bite.

**Matthew Sleeth, MD**
**Executive Director of Blessed Earth**
**Lexington, Kentucky**

## Questions _____

What would a perfect sabbath day look like for you, and how close are your current Sabbath practices to this ideal?

Why is the longest of the Ten Commandments the one we feel most comfortable ignoring?

What are the consequences when you, your family, and your church are on the go, 24/7?

## Prayer _____

Lord of the sabbath, teach us peace. Prince of peace, teach us to sabbath. You rest; you are holy. Therefore, teach us to rest in your holiness. Shabbat shalom. *Amen.*

## Luke 6:27-49

27"But I say to you that listen, Love your enemies, do good to those who hate you, 28bless those who curse you, pray for those who abuse you. 29If anyone strikes you on the cheek, offer the other also; and from anyone who takes away your coat do not withhold even your shirt. 30Give to everyone who begs from you; and if anyone takes away your goods, do not ask for them again. 31Do to others as you would have them do to you. 32"If you love those who love you, what credit is that to you? For even sinners love those who love them. 33If you do good to those who do good to you, what credit is that to you? For even sinners do the same. 34If you lend to those from whom you hope to receive, what credit is that to you? Even sinners lend to sinners, to receive as much again. 35But love your enemies, do good, and lend, expecting nothing in return. Your reward will be great, and you will be children of the Most High; for he is kind to the ungrateful and the wicked. 36Be merciful, just as your Father is merciful.

37"Do not judge, and you will not be judged; do not condemn, and you will not be condemned. Forgive, and you will be forgiven; 38give, and it will be given to you. A good measure, pressed down, shaken together, running over, will be put into your lap; for the measure you give will be the measure you get back." 39He also told them a parable: "Can a blind person guide a blind person? Will not both fall into a pit? 40A disciple is not above the teacher, but everyone who is fully qualified will be like the teacher. 41Why do you see the speck in your neighbor's eye, but do not notice the log in your own eye? <sup>42</sup>Or how can you say to your neighbor, 'Friend, let me take out the speck in your eye,' when you yourself do not see the log in your own eye? You hypocrite, first take the log out of your own eye, and then you will see clearly to take the speck out of your neighbor's eye. <sup>43</sup>"No good tree bears bad fruit, nor again does a bad tree bear good fruit; <sup>44</sup>for each tree is known by its own fruit. Figs are not gathered from thorns, nor are grapes picked from a bramble bush. <sup>45</sup>The good person out of the good treasure of the heart produces good, and the evil person out of evil treasure produces evil; for it is out of the abundance of the heart that the mouth speaks. <sup>46</sup>"Why do you call me 'Lord, Lord,' and do not do what I tell you? <sup>47</sup>I will show you what someone is like who comes to me, hears my words, and acts on them. <sup>48</sup>That one is like a man building a house, who dug deeply and laid the foundation on rock; when a flood arose, the river burst against that house but could not shake it, because it had been well built. <sup>49</sup>But the one who hears and does not act is like a man who built a house on the ground without a foundation. When the river burst against it, immediately it fell, and great was the ruin of that house."

# Reflection

Working from the assumption that you address a matter only when necessary, we can infer that people were not acting in the way that Jesus called for. Otherwise, he would not need to exhort them about their behavior. We can say that the people of his day were normal. They loved those who loved them. They held on tightly to what they believed belonged to them. They judged one another. They said one thing and did another. Surely, there must have been some people who behaved differently from those Jesus criticized. However, they were probably far fewer in number than the rest.

We gravitate toward, accept, feel safe around, and love people who are most like us. This is normal human behavior. It is perfectly understandable. Most of us were raised to behave this way. Don't trust strangers!

What Jesus challenges us to do is to move beyond our normal safe behavior and open ourselves to the stranger(s). He calls us to enlarge our circle of acceptable people. (It seems to me that the circle has shrunk over the years.)

In other words, Jesus calls us to become like God, who causes the rain to fall and the sun to shine upon all people. Jesus calls us to be the people who are made in the image of God—and to be people who see all others as being made in the same image. He calls us to go beyond the normal. He calls us to be the divine presence in the world.

**The Rt. Rev. Scott Hayashi**
**Bishop of the Diocese of Utah**
**Salt Lake City, Utah**

## Questions

Whom do you find to be most threatening or hard to love?

Who demonstrated to you by their life that God was real?

## Prayer

I pray to you, O God, that my life may be a witness to your saving mercy. May I become more, not less, dependent upon you for all things, in order that in my dependency upon you, I may be a witness to your love in this world. *Amen.*

heard this, including the tax collectors, acknowledged the justice of God, because they had been baptized with John's baptism. <sup>30</sup>But by refusing to be baptized by him, the Pharisees and the lawyers rejected God's purpose for themselves.) <sup>31</sup>"To what then will I compare the people of this generation, and what are they like? <sup>32</sup>They are like children sitting in the marketplace and calling to one another, 'We played the flute for you, and you did not dance; we wailed, and you did not weep.' <sup>33</sup>For John the Baptist has come eating no bread and drinking no wine, and you say, 'He has a demon'; <sup>34</sup>the Son of Man has come eating and drinking, and you say, 'Look, a glutton and a drunkard, a friend of tax collectors and sinners!' <sup>35</sup>Nevertheless, wisdom is vindicated by all her children."

# Reflection

In Luke, John the Baptist was arrested around the time Jesus arrived to be baptized. He was, let us say, taken off the scene to clear the stage for Jesus. John warned of the coming wrath that would clear the threshing floor. Later, in prison, John was in turmoil. Jesus, the person who was gaining attention, was not fulfilling what John had prophesied. From birth, John's whole life had been dedicated to one cause. And now, close to his end, he asks, "Are you the one who is to come, or are we to wait for another?"

John had not been wrong about God sending "one who is more powerful than I..." But his conception of that "one" was inaccurate. In prison, he holds to his conception. "Are we to wait for another?" If Jesus was the one it would mean that John got it wrong. His whole life, the strings that held it all together, would come undone. His passion and fury were fueled by his desires for what he thought God should do. But God was up to something else.

And that something else? That was Jesus.

**The Rt. Rev. Scott Hayashi**
**Bishop of the Diocese of Utah**
**Salt Lake City, Utah**

## Questions

How much of your vision is based on your desires?

How can you tell if what you want is what God wants?

What is God up to with you?

## Prayer

O God, my God, let it be your will, not mine. Let my eyes see your vision and not my own. May you so fill me that all I do and say will be what you desire. And always, O God, to your honor and glory. *Amen.*

## Luke 7:36-50

36One of the Pharisees asked Jesus to eat with him, and he went into the Pharisee's house and took his place at the table. 37And a woman in the city, who was a sinner, having learned that he was eating in the Pharisee's house, brought an alabaster jar of ointment. 38She stood behind him at his feet, weeping, and began to bathe his feet with her tears and to dry them with her hair. Then she continued kissing his feet and anointing them with the ointment. 39Now when the Pharisee who had invited him saw it, he said to himself, "If this man were a prophet, he would have known who and what kind of woman this is who is touching him—that she is a sinner." 40Jesus spoke up and said to him, "Simon, I have something to say to you." "Teacher," he replied, "Speak." 41"A certain creditor had two debtors; one owed five hundred denarii, and the other fifty. 42When they could not pay, he canceled the debts for both of them. Now which of them will love him more?" 43Simon answered, "I suppose the one for whom he canceled the greater debt." And Jesus said to him, "You have judged rightly." 44Then turning toward the woman, he said to Simon, "Do you see this woman? I entered your house; you gave me no water for my feet, but she has bathed my feet with her tears and dried them with her hair. 45You gave me no kiss, but from the time I came in she has not stopped kissing my feet. 46You did not anoint my head with oil, but she has anointed my feet with ointment. 47Therefore, I tell you, her sins, which were many, have been forgiven; hence she has shown great love.

But the one to whom little is forgiven, loves little." [48]Then he said to her, "Your sins are forgiven." [49]But those who were at the table with him began to say among themselves, "Who is this who even forgives sins?" [50]And he said to the woman, "Your faith has saved you; go in peace."

# Reflection

I saw the movie *Captain Phillips* last night. A middle-aged sea captain from Vermont is sailing a cargo ship that is hijacked by Somali pirates. The captain succeeds in getting the pirates to take the cash and escape in a lifeboat, but when they are about to depart, the pirates decide to take the captain with them.

So this middle-aged white guy from Vermont finds himself in a tiny enclosed space with four Somali pirates, young men who are high on khat (a leaf that they chew that has narcotic properties) and half-starved in appearance. His life hangs in the balance as dehydration sets in, and the young men, who are heavily armed, begin to fight.

The captain is rescued and brought aboard a navy ship where he is examined by a female nurse. When she tells him the simple words, "You are safe," he begins to cry hysterically. He thanks her over and over again and can hardly speak.

We do not know who the female "sinner" was in Luke's gospel. Was she raped? Was she traumatized in some way? Had she stolen something or had a child of hers died? Whatever happened to her, whatever she did, it must have been traumatic, because when she sees Jesus, she breaks down and cries. She must have realized that she was safe. She keeps crying, her tears wetting his feet, which she dries with her hair.

Only those who have known pain and darkness can ever be truly grateful for the light. To live in comfort and peace is wonderful, but how can you fully appreciate what it means to be forgiven, to be safe from your own sins and the sins of others, if you have never known what it means to struggle? It is those who suffer who know best what it means to be healed. It is those who know danger and darkness who can understand the gift of safety. It is the sinner who can best understand the immense grace that is given to us through God's forgiveness.

**The Very Rev. Kate Moorehead**
**Dean of St. John's Cathedral**
**Jacksonville, Florida**

## Questions

What do you think happened to this woman?

How do you imagine that she came to find Jesus?

What are the times in your life when you have struggled, and how have these experiences brought you closer to God?

## Prayer

Almighty God, we come to you on our knees like this lost woman. We look back upon our lives, and we can see times when we were lost without you. Thank you for restoring us to your grace and mercy. Thank you for weaknesses that can bring us to our knees, and guide us to acknowledge our dependence on you alone. Help us always to remember that it is only by your grace that we can become well and whole. *Amen.*

## Luke 8:1-25

8 Soon afterwards he went on through cities and villages, proclaiming and bringing the good news of the kingdom of God. The twelve were with him, ²as well as some women who had been cured of evil spirits and infirmities: Mary, called Magdalene, from whom seven demons had gone out, ³and Joanna, the wife of Herod's steward Chuza, and Susanna, and many others, who provided for them out of their resources.

⁴When a great crowd gathered and people from town after town came to him, he said in a parable: ⁵"A sower went out to sow his seed; and as he sowed, some fell on the path and was trampled on, and the birds of the air ate it up. ⁶Some fell on the rock; and as it grew up, it withered for lack of moisture. ⁷Some fell among thorns, and the thorns grew with it and choked it. ⁸Some fell into good soil, and when it grew, it produced a hundredfold." As he said this, he called out, "Let anyone with ears to hear listen!" ⁹Then his disciples asked him what this parable meant. ¹⁰He said, "To you it has been given to know the secrets of the kingdom of God; but to others I speak in parables, so that 'looking they may not perceive, and listening they may not understand.' ¹¹"Now the parable is this: The seed is the word of God. ¹²The ones on the path are those who have heard; then the devil comes and takes away the word from their hearts, so that they may not believe and be saved. ¹³The ones on the rock are those who, when they hear the word, receive it with joy. But these have no root; they

believe only for a while and in a time of testing fall away. [14]As for what fell among the thorns, these are the ones who hear; but as they go on their way, they are choked by the cares and riches and pleasures of life, and their fruit does not mature. [15]But as for that in the good soil, these are the ones who, when they hear the word, hold it fast in an honest and good heart, and bear fruit with patient endurance. [16]"No one after lighting a lamp hides it under a jar, or puts it under a bed, but puts it on a lampstand, so that those who enter may see the light. [17]For nothing is hidden that will not be disclosed, nor is anything secret that will not become known and come to light. [18]Then pay attention to how you listen; for to those who have, more will be given; and from those who do not have, even what they seem to have will be taken away." [19]Then his mother and his brothers came to him, but they could not reach him because of the crowd. [20]And he was told, "Your mother and your brothers are standing outside, wanting to see you." [21]But he said to them, "My mother and my brothers are those who hear the word of God and do it."

[22]One day he got into a boat with his disciples, and he said to them, "Let us go across to the other side of the lake." So they put out, [23]and while they were sailing he fell asleep. A windstorm swept down on the lake, and the boat was filling with water, and they were in danger. [24]They went to him and woke him up, shouting, "Master, Master, we are perishing!" And he woke up and rebuked the wind and the raging waves; they ceased, and there was a calm. [25]He said to them, "Where is your faith?" They were afraid and amazed, and said to one another, "Who then is this, that he commands even the winds and the water, and they obey him?"

# Reflection

Jesus must have been exhausted. After calling some of his greatest women followers, he teaches an incredible parable to a large crowd on the shore, gets into a boat, and then falls into a deep sleep while the disciples sail away to the other side of the sea of Galilee.

I have a large picture over the desk in my office. It is a picture of the sea of Galilee. I took the picture when I was just finishing seminary. My husband and I spent almost a month backpacking in Israel, and on our final night, I took a beautiful picture just as the sun was setting.

There are two mountains off the shore of the sea that cross in a particular way, making a funnel for the wind to gain force. It is called the Valley of the Doves. If the wind blows in a certain way, it can cause a storm to pick up on the sea within minutes. It is rather alarming how quick the entire process can be. One moment, you are sailing calmly, and the next, you are being blown about.

But isn't that just like our lives? One moment, things are smooth and easy and then a diagnosis comes or your teenager gets in a car accident or your spouse tells you of doubts about your marriage. One moment, everything seems good, and the next moment, it all seems to go to hell in a handbasket.

But Jesus never panics. He doesn't buy into the hysteria. He simply asks them, "Where is your faith?" Our lives are full of unpredictable waves and weather, but beneath all of that, there is this steady presence of Christ. Remember that he is in the boat with the disciples the entire time. And Christ is with you in the storms of your life.

When you ask for his help, he will calm the sea effortlessly, and he will ask you, Why are you so afraid?

**The Very Rev. Kate Moorehead**
**Dean of St. John's Cathedral**
**Jacksonville, Florida**

## Questions _____

Why was Jesus so tired? Imagine what his life was like each day.

When have storms come up suddenly in your life? Have you become afraid?

How can we trust that Jesus is with us on stormy seas?

## Prayer _____

Lord of all, you made the heavens and the earth. You created the sea and all that is in it. You made the calm and you made the storm. Help us to become aware of your presence especially in the crazy times of our lives, when the winds pick up speed and things feel out of control. Give us a deep and abiding awareness of your peace that passes all human understanding. This we ask in the name of Jesus our Lord. *Amen.*

## Luke 8:26-56

²⁶Then they arrived at the country of the Gerasenes, which is opposite Galilee. ²⁷As he stepped out on land, a man of the city who had demons met him. For a long time he had worn no clothes, and he did not live in a house but in the tombs. ²⁸When he saw Jesus, he fell down before him and shouted at the top of his voice, "What have you to do with me, Jesus, Son of the Most High God? I beg you, do not torment me"— ²⁹for Jesus had commanded the unclean spirit to come out of the man. (For many times it had seized him; he was kept under guard and bound with chains and shackles, but he would break the bonds and be driven by the demon into the wilds.) ³⁰Jesus then asked him, "What is your name?" He said, "Legion"; for many demons had entered him. ³¹They begged him not to order them to go back into the abyss. ³²Now there on the hillside a large herd of swine was feeding; and the demons begged Jesus to let them enter these. So he gave them permission. ³³Then the demons came out of the man and entered the swine, and the herd rushed down the steep bank into the lake and was drowned. ³⁴When the swineherds saw what had happened, they ran off and told it in the city and in the country. ³⁵Then people came out to see what had happened, and when they came to Jesus, they found the man from whom the demons had gone sitting at the feet of Jesus, clothed and in his right mind. And they were afraid. ³⁶Those who had seen it told them how the one who had been possessed by demons had been healed. ³⁷Then all the people of the surrounding country of the Gerasenes asked

Jesus to leave them; for they were seized with great fear. So he got into the boat and returned. [38]The man from whom the demons had gone begged that he might be with him; but Jesus sent him away, saying, [39]"Return to your home, and declare how much God has done for you." So he went away, proclaiming throughout the city how much Jesus had done for him.

[40]Now when Jesus returned, the crowd welcomed him, for they were all waiting for him. [41]Just then there came a man named Jairus, a leader of the synagogue. He fell at Jesus' feet and begged him to come to his house, [42]for he had an only daughter, about twelve years old, who was dying. As he went, the crowds pressed in on him. [43]Now there was a woman who had been suffering from hemorrhages for twelve years; and though she had spent all she had on physicians, no one could cure her. [44]She came up behind him and touched the fringe of his clothes, and immediately her hemorrhage stopped. [45]Then Jesus asked, "Who touched me?" When all denied it, Peter said, "Master, the crowds surround you and press in on you." [46]But Jesus said, "Someone touched me; for I noticed that power had gone out from me." [47]When the woman saw that she could not remain hidden, she came trembling; and falling down before him, she declared in the presence of all the people why she had touched him, and how she had been immediately healed. [48]He said to her, "Daughter, your faith has made you well; go in peace." [49]While he was still speaking, someone came from the leader's house to say, "Your daughter is dead; do not trouble the teacher any longer." [50]When Jesus heard this, he replied, "Do not fear. Only believe, and she will be saved." [51]When he came to the house, he did not allow anyone to enter with him, except Peter, John, and James, and the child's father and mother.

[52]They were all weeping and wailing for her; but he said, "Do not weep; for she is not dead but sleeping." [53]And they laughed at him, knowing that she was dead. [54]But he took her by the hand and called out, "Child, get up!" [55]Her spirit returned, and she got up at once. Then he directed them to give her something to eat. [56]Her parents were astounded; but he ordered them to tell no one what had happened.

# Reflection

A lot takes place in these thirty verses, but it's the crowd's erratic actions that stay with me.

The crowd is the connective tissue of this passage, a roiling and unpredictable gaggle who come out to see what had happened to the Gerasene demoniac and who end up demanding Jesus leave when they see that the one they had chained was indeed healed. Another crowd gathers to welcome Jesus when he returns to Galilee and presses in on him with such force that a woman, hemorrhaging for years, sees her chance to touch the fringe of Jesus' robe. Yet another crowd weeps and wails over the death of Jairus' daughter, but they jeer when Jesus insists that "she is not dead but sleeping."

What an erratic character, this crowd! Such a crowd is just as likely to be singing "Hosanna" as nailing an innocent man to the cross.

Jesus and the people he encounters stand out from the crowd, albeit for different reasons. Jesus is distinguished by his inquisitive nature: "What is your name?" "Who touched me?" and by his direct manner of speaking: "Get up." In contrast, the individuals Jesus encounters stand out because of their undisguised need: the demoniac falls down on his knees and shouts out; Jairus begs Jesus to come to his house; and the hemorrhaging woman, who also kept her eye on the crowd, saw her chance and reached out.

Miguel Escobar
Senior Program Director of Leadership Resources
Episcopal Church Foundation
New York, New York

## Questions _____

Today's "crowd" is only a click of a mouse away. Through Facebook, Twitter, and other social media, we can now see the erratic nature of a crowd that rejects, welcomes, presses in on, weeps, and laughs at anything and everything. Who are we in the midst of this crowd? When do we join in?

How might we be like Christ, insisting on quiet questioning, direct action, and simple words?

How might we break from the crowd by sharing with God our undisguised need?

## Prayer _____

The Gerasene demoniac, Jairus, and the hemorrhaging woman had such profound need that they dared step out of the crowd for a direct encounter with you. Jesus, help us to see our own need as an impetus for encountering you and daring to step out of the crowd to touch the fringe of your robe. *Amen.*

## Luke 9:1-27

9 Then Jesus called the twelve together and gave them power and authority over all demons and to cure diseases, ²and he sent them out to proclaim the kingdom of God and to heal. ³He said to them, "Take nothing for your journey, no staff, nor bag, nor bread, nor money—not even an extra tunic. ⁴Whatever house you enter, stay there, and leave from there. ⁵Wherever they do not welcome you, as you are leaving that town shake the dust off your feet as a testimony against them." ⁶They departed and went through the villages, bringing the good news and curing diseases everywhere. ⁷Now Herod the ruler heard about all that had taken place, and he was perplexed, because it was said by some that John had been raised from the dead, ⁸by some that Elijah had appeared, and by others that one of the ancient prophets had arisen. ⁹Herod said, "John I beheaded; but who is this about whom I hear such things?" And he tried to see him.

¹⁰On their return the apostles told Jesus all they had done. He took them with him and withdrew privately to a city called Bethsaida. ¹¹When the crowds found out about it, they followed him; and he welcomed them, and spoke to them about the kingdom of God, and healed those who needed to be cured. ¹²The day was drawing to a close, and the twelve came to him and said, "Send the crowd away, so that they may go into the surrounding villages and countryside, to lodge and get provisions; for we are here in a deserted place." ¹³But he said to them, "You give them something to eat." They said, "We have no

more than five loaves and two fish—unless we are to go and buy food for all these people." ¹⁴For there were about five thousand men. And he said to his disciples, "Make them sit down in groups of about fifty each." ¹⁵They did so and made them all sit down. ¹⁶And taking the five loaves and the two fish, he looked up to heaven, and blessed and broke them, and gave them to the disciples to set before the crowd. ¹⁷And all ate and were filled. What was left over was gathered up, twelve baskets of broken pieces.

¹⁸Once when Jesus was praying alone, with only the disciples near him, he asked them, "Who do the crowds say that I am?" ¹⁹They answered, "John the Baptist; but others, Elijah; and still others, that one of the ancient prophets has arisen." ²⁰He said to them, "But who do you say that I am?" Peter answered, "The Messiah of God." ²¹He sternly ordered and commanded them not to tell anyone, ²²saying, "The Son of Man must undergo great suffering, and be rejected by the elders, chief priests, and scribes, and be killed, and on the third day be raised." ²³Then he said to them all, "If any want to become my followers, let them deny themselves and take up their cross daily and follow me. ²⁴For those who want to save their life will lose it, and those who lose their life for my sake will save it. ²⁵What does it profit them if they gain the whole world, but lose or forfeit themselves? ²⁶Those who are ashamed of me and of my words, of them the Son of Man will be ashamed when he comes in his glory and the glory of the Father and of the holy angels. ²⁷But truly I tell you, there are some standing here who will not taste death before they see the kingdom of God."

# Reflection

A lot of attention is paid to what Jesus tells the twelve they are to do ("to proclaim the kingdom of God and to heal"), and the minimalist method he tells them to use while doing it ("Take nothing for your journey…"). But here's the odd thing about this passage: the twelve are sent out, they return just four verses later, and Luke offers just a one-line sketch of what they encountered on the way. "They departed and went through the villages, bringing the good news and curing diseases everywhere."

How long were the twelve gone for? Which villages did they visit? Who and what did they encounter along the way? When the disciples return, they diligently tell Jesus all they had done, but I remain curious about how they evolved while out there on the road. What did Jesus' simple method of coming and going help them to understand more deeply?

When they return, it is clear that the twelve now see things that others do not. When Jesus feeds the five thousand, the crowd is ready to proclaim Jesus as Elijah, a reference to the Old Testament leader who performed a similar miraculous feeding. "Who do the crowds say that I am?" Jesus asks, "But who do you say that I am?" It's telling that only now is Peter prepared to offer a different answer.

"The Messiah of God," Peter proclaims, perhaps saying aloud for the first time something he had been mulling over while out there on the road.

**Miguel Escobar**
**Senior Program Director of Leadership Resources**
**Episcopal Church Foundation**
**New York City, New York**

## Questions_____

Think about the manner in which you are proclaiming the kingdom. Is it as bare bones as that which Jesus describes? Is it a rather luxurious affair or does it include, as Jesus insists, simplicity and the cross?

Where and when did you come to realize Jesus as Messiah?

## Prayer _____

Loving God, strip us of our pretensions. Rid us of our boring need for worldly comfort and our constant seeking after praise. Take us on a journey where we will go from distraction to discipleship, from superficiality to deep Christ-like living for others. And, in doing so, help us to know who you are more deeply. *Amen.*

## Luke 9:28-62

²⁸Now about eight days after these sayings Jesus took with him Peter and John and James, and went up on the mountain to pray. ²⁹And while he was praying, the appearance of his face changed, and his clothes became dazzling white. ³⁰Suddenly they saw two men, Moses and Elijah, talking to him. ³¹They appeared in glory and were speaking of his departure, which he was about to accomplish at Jerusalem. ³²Now Peter and his companions were weighed down with sleep; but since they had stayed awake, they saw his glory and the two men who stood with him. ³³Just as they were leaving him, Peter said to Jesus, "Master, it is good for us to be here; let us make three dwellings, one for you, one for Moses, and one for Elijah"—not knowing what he said. ³⁴While he was saying this, a cloud came and overshadowed them; and they were terrified as they entered the cloud. ³⁵Then from the cloud came a voice that said, "This is my Son, my Chosen; listen to him!" ³⁶When the voice had spoken, Jesus was found alone. And they kept silent and in those days told no one any of the things they had seen.

³⁷On the next day, when they had come down from the mountain, a great crowd met him. ³⁸Just then a man from the crowd shouted, "Teacher, I beg you to look at my son; he is my only child. ³⁹Suddenly a spirit seizes him, and all at once he shrieks. It convulses him until he foams at the mouth; it mauls him and will scarcely leave him. ⁴⁰I begged your disciples to cast it out, but they could not." ⁴¹Jesus answered, "You faithless

and perverse generation, how much longer must I be with you and bear with you? Bring your son here." <sup>42</sup>While he was coming, the demon dashed him to the ground in convulsions. But Jesus rebuked the unclean spirit, healed the boy, and gave him back to his father.

<sup>43</sup>And all were astounded at the greatness of God. While everyone was amazed at all that he was doing, he said to his disciples, <sup>44</sup>"Let these words sink into your ears: The Son of Man is going to be betrayed into human hands." <sup>45</sup>But they did not understand this saying; its meaning was concealed from them, so that they could not perceive it. And they were afraid to ask him about this saying. <sup>46</sup>An argument arose among them as to which one of them was the greatest. <sup>47</sup>But Jesus, aware of their inner thoughts, took a little child and put it by his side, <sup>48</sup>and said to them, "Whoever welcomes this child

in my name welcomes me, and whoever welcomes me welcomes the one who sent me; for the least among all of you is the greatest." <sup>49</sup>John answered, "Master, we saw someone casting out demons in your name, and we tried to stop him, because he does not follow with us." <sup>50</sup>But Jesus said to him, "Do not stop him; for whoever is not against you is for you."

<sup>51</sup>When the days drew near for him to be taken up, he set his face to go to Jerusalem. <sup>52</sup>And he sent messengers ahead of him. On their way they entered a village of the Samaritans to make ready for him; <sup>53</sup>but they did not receive him, because his face was set toward Jerusalem. <sup>54</sup>When his disciples James and John saw it, they said, "Lord, do you want us to command fire to come down from heaven and consume them?" <sup>55</sup>But he turned and rebuked them. <sup>56</sup>Then they went on to another village.

⁵⁷As they were going along the road, someone said to him, "I will follow you wherever you go." ⁵⁸And Jesus said to him, "Foxes have holes, and birds of the air have nests; but the Son of Man has nowhere to lay his head." ⁵⁹To another he said, "Follow me." But he said, "Lord, first let me go and bury my father." ⁶⁰But Jesus said to him, "Let the dead bury their own dead; but as for you, go and proclaim the kingdom of God." ⁶¹Another said, "I will follow you, Lord; but let me first say farewell to those at my home." ⁶²Jesus said to him, "No one who puts a hand to the plow and looks back is fit for the kingdom of God."

# Reflection

Churches are named for them. Statues and paintings have been crafted in their honor. They are Christianity's revered pioneers, heroes of the Church, the apostles. And yet they, like we, often missed the mark. They, like we, failed. Nowhere do we see this more clearly than in the ninth chapter of Luke's Gospel, in this series of brief vignettes.

The disciples are unable to cast out the possessing demon. They fail to understand when Jesus speaks to them of betrayal and suffering, and they lack the courage to ask him to explain. They argue about who among them is the greatest. They protest about someone outside their number who is casting out demons in Jesus' name, doing the very thing that they themselves failed to do. And when a Samaritan village refuses to welcome Jesus, they call for deadly retribution against the villagers, only to be rebuked by Jesus. Again and again throughout this section, these revered heroes fail and fall, and end up with egg on their faces.

This takes place after being commissioned at the start of the chapter and after three of them had witnessed Jesus in transfigured glory! But the good news is that through these same flawed, fallible, far-from-ideal pioneers, God changed the world.

On those days when I see myself as flawed, when I feel fallible and far from ideal, I can take heart in knowing that the God of fresh starts is able to change the world again, through me, through you, and through us.

**The Rev. C. K. Robertson**
**Canon to the Presiding Bishop**
**New York City, New York**

*A Journey with Luke*

## Question

Think of someone you know who has failed or fallen, and consider what you can say or do to reach out and encourage that person. Who comes to mind?

## Prayer

O God of grace, forgive me for my failings and for anything that keeps me from being all that I can be for you and for the world. Give me strength to put my hand to the plow and help change the world, for Jesus' sake. *Amen.*

## Luke 10:1-20

**10** After this the Lord appointed seventy others and sent them on ahead of him in pairs to every town and place where he himself intended to go. ²He said to them, "The harvest is plentiful, but the laborers are few; therefore ask the Lord of the harvest to send out laborers into his harvest. ³Go on your way. See, I am sending you out like lambs into the midst of wolves. ⁴Carry no purse, no bag, no sandals; and greet no one on the road. ⁵Whatever house you enter, first say, 'Peace to this house!' ⁶And if anyone is there who shares in peace, your peace will rest on that person; but if not, it will return to you. ⁷Remain in the same house, eating and drinking whatever they provide, for the laborer deserves to be paid. Do not move about from house to house. ⁸Whenever you enter a town and its people welcome you, eat what is set before you; ⁹cure the sick who are there, and say to them, 'The kingdom of God has come near to you.' ¹⁰But whenever you enter a town and they do not welcome you, go out into its streets and say, ¹¹'Even the dust of your town that clings to our feet, we wipe off in protest against you. Yet know this: the kingdom of God has come near.' ¹²I tell you, on that day it will be more tolerable for Sodom than for that town. ¹³"Woe to you, Chorazin! Woe to you, Bethsaida! For if the deeds of power done in you had been done in Tyre and Sidon, they would have repented long ago, sitting in sackcloth and ashes. ¹⁴But at the judgment it will be more tolerable for Tyre and Sidon than for you. ¹⁵And you, Capernaum, will you be exalted to heaven? No, you will be brought down to Hades. [16]"Whoever listens to you listens to me, and whoever rejects you rejects me, and whoever rejects me rejects the one who sent me."

[17]The seventy returned with joy, saying, "Lord, in your name even the demons submit to us!" [18]He said to them, "I watched Satan fall from heaven like a flash of lightning. [19]See, I have given you authority to tread on snakes and scorpions, and over all the power of the enemy; and nothing will hurt you. [20]Nevertheless, do not rejoice at this, that the spirits submit to you, but rejoice that your names are written in heaven."

# Reflection

Seventy others. Just one chapter after Jesus commissions the twelve apostles, we find him commissioning another numbered group. The number seventy is significant, with its roots in the book of Numbers (11:16-17). There, Moses admits to God that he can no longer carry the burden of leadership alone. God tells him to select seventy elders to share the burden and empowers them with the same spirit that filled Moses. Now Luke tells a tale of seventy unnamed disciples who are sent out by Jesus to work in the harvest.

It is a remarkable tale, unique to Luke, one that presages his Gospel sequel, the Acts of the Apostles. In Acts, we encounter others like the seventy—Paul and Barnabas, Priscilla and Aquila, Phoebe, Lydia, Silas and Timothy, and more—who share the apostolic task and take it further, from Jerusalem to the ends of the earth.

The story of the seventy, and the story of all those other workers introduced later in Acts, is our story. We may not be the twelve, we may not be bishops and archbishops, famous leaders, or household names, but we are called, commissioned, and empowered for service just the same. The harvest is indeed too plentiful to leave it solely to a small, elite group of professionals. No, the harvest, the task, the calling, is for us as well. We are the seventy, and Jesus is sending us out.

The Rev. C. K. Robertson
Canon to the Presiding Bishop
New York City, New York

## Questions

Think of your own spiritual family tree: who are some of the people who have shown you the love of God, who have carried the message of Jesus to you?

Who are some people to whom God might be sending you?

## Prayer

O God of power, fill us with your Spirit, that we might spread your message and share your love with all those we encounter, this day and every day, in the name of Jesus, who calls us and sends us forth as faithful witnesses. *Amen.*

## Luke 10:21-42

²¹At that same hour Jesus rejoiced in the Holy Spirit and said, "I thank you, Father, Lord of heaven and earth, because you have hidden these things from the wise and the intelligent and have revealed them to infants; yes, Father, for such was your gracious will. ²²All things have been handed over to me by my Father; and no one knows who the Son is except the Father, or who the Father is except the Son and anyone to whom the Son chooses to reveal him." ²³Then turning to the disciples, Jesus said to them privately, "Blessed are the eyes that see what you see! ²⁴For I tell you that many prophets and kings desired to see what you see, but did not see it, and to hear what you hear, but did not hear it."

²⁵Just then a lawyer stood up to test Jesus. "Teacher," he said, "what must I do to inherit eternal life?" ²⁶He said to him, "What is written in the law? What do you read there?" ²⁷He answered, "You shall love the Lord your God with all your heart, and with all your soul, and with all your strength, and with all your mind; and your neighbor as yourself." ²⁸And he said to him, "You have given the right answer; do this, and you will live." ²⁹But wanting to justify himself, he asked Jesus, "And who is my neighbor?" ³⁰Jesus replied, "A man was going down from Jerusalem to Jericho, and fell into the hands of robbers, who stripped him, beat him, and went away, leaving him half dead. ³¹Now by chance a priest was going down that road; and when he saw him, he passed by on the other side. ³²So likewise a Levite, when he came to the

place and saw him, passed by on the other side. ³³But a Samaritan while traveling came near him; and when he saw him, he was moved with pity. ³⁴He went to him and bandaged his wounds, having poured oil and wine on them. Then he put him on his own animal, brought him to an inn, and took care of him. ³⁵The next day he took out two denarii, gave them to the innkeeper, and said, 'Take care of him; and when I come back, I will repay you whatever more you spend.' ³⁶Which of these three, do you think, was a neighbor to the man who fell into the hands of the robbers?" ³⁷He said, "The one who showed him mercy." Jesus said to him, "Go and do likewise."

³⁸Now as they went on their way, he entered a certain village, where a woman named Martha welcomed him into her home. ³⁹She had a sister named Mary, who sat at the Lord's feet and listened to what he was saying. ⁴⁰But Martha was distracted by her many tasks; so she came to him and asked, "Lord, do you not care that my sister has left me to do all the work by myself? Tell her then to help me." ⁴¹But the Lord answered her, "Martha, Martha, you are worried and distracted by many things; ⁴²there is need of only one thing. Mary has chosen the better part, which will not be taken away from her."

# Reflection

Jesus rejoices in the Holy Spirit at the return of his disciples from their first missionary journey. The commission he has received from his Father has started well. Jesus' followers are beginning to learn what he has to teach them. In this passage, we have one famous story and one well-known anecdote that are meant to further their understanding of true discipleship.

The lawyer presses Jesus the rabbi to expand on the law to love one's neighbor as oneself and is given in reply the parable of the Good Samaritan. The act of practical care by a stranger who is outside the Law demonstrates that it is not religious identity but loving action that makes one a true disciple.

Then, having told this story, Jesus arrives at the home of Martha, one of his closest friends, and one of the first people to recognize him as the Messiah (John 11:27). Her younger sister Mary seats herself with the other disciples around him on the floor to listen to his teaching. This time Jesus commends the student who listens and learns but leaves the necessary tasks of hospitality to the somewhat exasperated Martha.

It seems that true discipleship calls us to a life of both contemplation and action. Attentive listening to Jesus will set us on the right path, but active care for our neighbor will be the fruit of our learning. Loving attention to God will form us into disciples who are lovingly attentive to everyone we meet, especially the marginalized.

**The Rev. Marjorie Brown**
**Vicar of St. Mary the Virgin, Primrose Hill**
**London, England**

## Questions _____

Are you more naturally inclined to be active or contemplative?

What do you need most in your discipleship journey right now? More time for listening and reflection or more practical attention to your neighbor?

## Prayer _____

Jesus our rabbi, help us to rejoice with you in the Holy Spirit by opening our hearts to hear the message of your Father's love and deepening our awareness of the needs of others. *Amen.*

## Luke 11:1-13

11 He was praying in a certain place, and after he had finished, one of his disciples said to him, "Lord, teach us to pray, as John taught his disciples." ²He said to them, "When you pray, say: Father, hallowed be your name. Your kingdom come. ³Give us each day our daily bread. ⁴And forgive us our sins, for we ourselves forgive everyone indebted to us. And do not bring us to the time of trial." ⁵And he said to them, "Suppose one of you has a friend, and you go to him at midnight and say to him, 'Friend, lend me three loaves of bread; ⁶for a friend of mine has arrived, and I have nothing to set before him.' ⁷And he answers from within, 'Do not bother me; the door has already been locked, and my children are with me in bed; I cannot get up and give you anything.' ⁸I tell you, even though he will not get up and give him anything because he is his friend, at least because of his persistence he will get up and give him whatever he needs. ⁹"So I say to you, Ask, and it will be given you; search, and you will find; knock, and the door will be opened for you. ¹⁰For everyone who asks receives, and everyone who searches finds, and for everyone who knocks, the door will be opened. ¹¹Is there anyone among you who, if your child asks for a fish, will give a snake instead of a fish? ¹²Or if the child asks for an egg, will give a scorpion? ¹³If you then, who are evil, know how to give good gifts to your children, how much more will the heavenly Father give the Holy Spirit to those who ask him!"

# Reflection

Jesus' relationship with his Father in heaven was obviously deeply attractive to his disciples. They wanted something like that for themselves, but they didn't know where to start. And if we are honest, we are in the same situation. Sitting or kneeling down to pray with a list of sins or petitions to present to God does not seem to bring us into the place of joy and refreshment that Jesus clearly experienced in his times of prayer.

No doubt the disciples hoped for some highly advanced and esoteric teaching that would enable them, the inner circle, to become spiritually adept. But what Jesus gave them was a form of prayer so simple that a young child could learn it by heart. The prayer addresses our most basic needs, for daily sustenance and protection from evil. It challenges us to pray for the coming of God's kingdom and to live by that hardest of all teachings, to love and forgive our enemies.

We will never become so advanced in our spiritual lives that we can move on from the Lord's Prayer. Jesus stresses that persistence in praying is what we most need to learn, not fancy techniques or flowery words. This prayer unites us with Jesus in his relationship with God, whom he teaches us to call Father with simple confidence. If we pray it faithfully, reflectively, trustingly alongside Jesus, we will learn more deeply that we are the children of a God who loves us and knows our needs.

**The Rev. Marjorie Brown**
**Vicar of St. Mary the Virgin, Primrose Hill**
**London, England**

## Question _____

Imagine that Jesus is sitting or kneeling beside you, saying aloud the words of the Lord's Prayer, and inviting you to say them with him. How does this change your experience of the prayer?

## Prayer _____

Lord, teach us to pray as you taught your disciples. Help us to make your words our own and to believe more and more deeply that, with you, we are truly the children of your loving heavenly Father. *Amen.*

## Luke 11:14-54

[14]Now he was casting out a demon that was mute; when the demon had gone out, the one who had been mute spoke, and the crowds were amazed. [15]But some of them said, "He casts out demons by Beelzebul, the ruler of the demons." [16]Others, to test him, kept demanding from him a sign from heaven. [17]But he knew what they were thinking and said to them, "Every kingdom divided against itself becomes a desert, and house falls on house. [18]If Satan also is divided against himself, how will his kingdom stand?—for you say that I cast out the demons by Beelzebul. [19]Now if I cast out the demons by Beelzebul, by whom do your exorcists cast them out? Therefore they will be your judges. [20]But if it is by the finger of God that I cast out the demons, then the kingdom of God has come to you. [21]When a strong man, fully armed, guards his castle, his property is safe. [22]But when one stronger than he attacks him and overpowers him, he takes away his armor in which he trusted and divides his plunder. [23]Whoever is not with me is against me, and whoever does not gather with me scatters. [24]"When the unclean spirit has gone out of a person, it wanders through waterless regions looking for a resting place, but not finding any, it says, 'I will return to my house from which I came.' [25]When it comes, it finds it swept and put in order. [26]Then it goes and brings seven other spirits more evil than itself, and they enter and live there; and the last state of that person is worse than the first."

[27]While he was saying this, a woman in the crowd raised her

voice and said to him, "Blessed is the womb that bore you and the breasts that nursed you!" [28]But he said, "Blessed rather are those who hear the word of God and obey it!"

[29]When the crowds were increasing, he began to say, "This generation is an evil generation; it asks for a sign, but no sign will be given to it except the sign of Jonah. [30]For just as Jonah became a sign to the people of Nineveh, so the Son of Man will be to this generation. [31]The queen of the South will rise at the judgment with the people of this generation and condemn them, because she came from the ends of the earth to listen to the wisdom of Solomon, and see, something greater than Solomon is here! [32]The people of Nineveh will rise up at the judgment with this generation and condemn it, because they repented at the proclamation of Jonah, and see, something greater than Jonah is here! [33]"No one after lighting a lamp puts it in a cellar, but on the lampstand so that those who enter may see the light. [34]Your eye is the lamp of your body. If your eye is healthy, your whole body is full of light; but if it is not healthy, your body is full of darkness. [35]Therefore consider whether the light in you is not darkness. [36]If then your whole body is full of light, with no part of it in darkness, it will be as full of light as when a lamp gives you light with its rays."

[37]While he was speaking, a Pharisee invited him to dine with him; so he went in and took his place at the table. [38]The Pharisee was amazed to see that he did not first wash before dinner. [39]Then the Lord said to him, "Now you Pharisees clean the outside of the cup and of the dish, but inside you are full of greed and wickedness. [40]You fools! Did not the one who made the outside make the inside also? [41]So give for alms those things that are within; and see, everything will be clean for you.

42"But woe to you Pharisees! For you tithe mint and rue and herbs of all kinds, and neglect justice and the love of God; it is these you ought to have practiced, without neglecting the others. 43Woe to you Pharisees! For you love to have the seat of honor in the synagogues and to be greeted with respect in the marketplaces. 44Woe to you! For you are like unmarked graves, and people walk over them without realizing it." 45One of the lawyers answered him, "Teacher, when you say these things, you insult us too." 46And he said, "Woe also to you lawyers! For you load people with burdens hard to bear, and you yourselves do not lift a finger to ease them. 47Woe to you! For you build the tombs of the prophets whom your ancestors killed. 48So you are witnesses and approve of the deeds of your ancestors; for they killed them, and you build their tombs. 49Therefore also the Wisdom of God said, 'I will send them prophets and apostles, some of whom they will kill and persecute,' 50so that this generation may be charged with the blood of all the prophets shed since the foundation of the world, 51from the blood of Abel to the blood of Zechariah, who perished between the altar and the sanctuary. Yes, I tell you, it will be charged against this generation. 52Woe to you lawyers! For you have taken away the key of knowledge; you did not enter yourselves, and you hindered those who were entering." 53When he went outside, the scribes and the Pharisees began to be very hostile toward him and to cross-examine him about many things, 54lying in wait for him, to catch him in something he might say.

# Reflection

Jesus' enemies assembled a long and thorough file on our Lord. Their dossier on him included unseemly exorcisms, Jesus' claim to fulfill biblical prophecy, and his regular and powerful denunciation of religious leaders for superficial teaching, narrowness, and hypocrisy. It's no wonder that these same leaders "began to be very hostile toward him…lying in wait for him, to catch him in something he might say." Even at this point in Jesus' ministry, as he slowly journeys to Jerusalem and his final confrontation with the forces of evil, the end is painfully clear. The outcome of Jesus' trial was determined long beforehand.

Yet Jesus does not devote his time to hiring a defense team or building a case for acquittal. Instead, he urges his followers to be vigilant against malignant spiritual powers and encourages a woman in the crowd to stick to the basics: "Blessed rather are those who hear the word of God and obey it!" Open your heart to the light, he says, and you will be transformed from the inside out. Jesus never wavers in his focus or allows himself to be distracted from his primary mission. He has good news to proclaim, even when the news has a hard edge, and he lets nothing turn him away from that essential task.

Nor should we. Jesus' commitment to his mission challenges us to examine our own call, to recognize the inevitable distractions that plague us, and to seek his strength to follow wherever he leads.

**The Rt. Rev. Edward S. Little II**
**Bishop of the Diocese of Northern Indiana**
**South Bend, Indiana**

## Questions _____

As Jesus preached and taught, many objected and sought to draw him into endless arguments. What are the voices—internal as well as external—that hinder us from discerning God's call?

How can we set aside distractions and focus more consciously on Jesus' invitation to hear and obey his word?

## Prayer _____

God our Father, give us hearts attuned to the voice of Jesus amid the many voices that clamor for our attention. May we receive your word with joy and commit ourselves afresh to the adventure of discipleship, for Jesus' sake. *Amen.*

## Luke 12:1-21

**12** Meanwhile, when the crowd gathered by the thousands, so that they trampled on one another, he began to speak first to his disciples, "Beware of the yeast of the Pharisees, that is, their hypocrisy. ²Nothing is covered up that will not be uncovered, and nothing secret that will not become known. ³Therefore whatever you have said in the dark will be heard in the light, and what you have whispered behind closed doors will be proclaimed from the housetops. ⁴"I tell you, my friends, do not fear those who kill the body, and after that can do nothing more. ⁵But I will warn you whom to fear: fear him who, after he has killed, has authority to cast into hell. Yes, I tell you, fear him! ⁶Are not five sparrows sold for two pennies? Yet not one of them is forgotten in God's sight. ⁷But even the hairs of your head are all counted. Do not be afraid; you are of more value than many sparrows. ⁸"And I tell you, everyone who acknowledges me before others, the Son of Man also will acknowledge before the angels of God; ⁹but whoever denies me before others will be denied before the angels of God. ¹⁰And everyone who speaks a word against the Son of Man will be forgiven; but whoever blasphemes against the Holy Spirit will not be forgiven. ¹¹When they bring you before the synagogues, the rulers, and the authorities, do not worry about how you are to defend yourselves or what you are to say; ¹²for the Holy Spirit will teach you at that very hour what you ought to say."

[13]Someone in the crowd said to him, "Teacher, tell my brother to divide the family inheritance with me." [14]But he said to him, "Friend, who set me to be a judge or arbitrator over you?" [15]And he said to them, "Take care! Be on your guard against all kinds of greed; for one's life does not consist in the abundance of possessions." [16]Then he told them a parable: "The land of a rich man produced abundantly. [17]And he thought to himself, 'What should I do, for I have no place to store my crops?' [18]Then he said, 'I will do this: I will pull down my barns and build larger ones, and there I will store all my grain and my goods. [19]And I will say to my soul, 'Soul, you have ample goods laid up for many years; relax, eat, drink, be merry.' [20]But God said to him, 'You fool! This very night your life is being demanded of you. And the things you have prepared, whose will they be?' [21]So it is with those who store up treasures for themselves but are not rich toward God."

# Reflection

Jesus' disciples have much to frighten them. "Beware of the yeast of the Pharisees," he warns them. False teaching, he says, can destroy your faith. "Do not fear those who kill the body, and after that can do nothing more." Yes, but that means that someone can kill your body! And when you're dragged before religious and political authorities, "do not worry about how you are to defend yourselves." This implies, of course, that the disciples were indeed stewing about how they might respond to persecution. Be careful, Jesus is telling his disciples (and us). This is a dangerous world.

Yet God has not left us to struggle alone. God's care for us is so complete that God minds the sparrows and numbers the hairs on our head. In the face of the most fearsome persecution, the Holy Spirit will give us supernatural wisdom. To be sure, Jesus warns us not to take prosperity for granted. The future is always, in human terms, uncertain. But even that warning is delivered in the wider setting of God's promises. When we place ourselves in Jesus' care, we have nothing ultimately to fear. The God of the universe is in charge of the big picture.

"Do not be afraid; you are of more value than many sparrows." The promise includes a command. Acknowledge me before others, Jesus says. Open your mouth when you're summoned into court, and the Spirit will speak through you. The antidote to fear, in other words, isn't to seek protection. Rather, and sometimes counter-intuitively, it's to obey Jesus.

**The Rt. Rev. Edward S. Little II**
**Bishop of the Diocese of Northern Indiana**
**South Bend, Indiana**

## Questions

While the challenges facing the disciples are significantly different than our own, the world remains a frightening place. What aspects of Christian discipleship do you find most fearsome?

What commands of Jesus give you pause?

What strategies have you adopted to overcome fear?

## Prayer

Lord God, in the midst of our fears, help us to keep our eyes fixed on Jesus, to listen for his voice, and to seek to do his will. Grant us to trust in your power as we obey Jesus' call. In his gracious name we pray. *Amen.*

## Luke 12:22-59

[22]He said to his disciples, "Therefore I tell you, do not worry about your life, what you will eat, or about your body, what you will wear. [23]For life is more than food, and the body more than clothing. [24]Consider the ravens: they neither sow nor reap, they have neither storehouse nor barn, and yet God feeds them. Of how much more value are you than the birds! [25]And can any of you by worrying add a single hour to your span of life? [26]If then you are not able to do so small a thing as that, why do you worry about the rest? [27]Consider the lilies, how they grow: they neither toil nor spin; yet I tell you, even Solomon in all his glory was not clothed like one of these. [28]But if God so clothes the grass of the field, which is alive today and tomorrow is thrown into the oven, how much more will he clothe you—you of little faith! [29]And do not keep striving for what you are to eat and what you are to drink, and do not keep worrying. [30]For it is the nations of the world that strive after all these things, and your Father knows that you need them. [31]Instead, strive for his kingdom, and these things will be given to you as well. [32]"Do not be afraid, little flock, for it is your Father's good pleasure to give you the kingdom. [33]Sell your possessions, and give alms. Make purses for yourselves that do not wear out, an unfailing treasure in heaven, where no thief comes near and no moth destroys. [34]For where your treasure is, there your heart will be also. [35]"Be dressed for action and have your lamps lit; [36]be like those who are waiting for their master to return from the wedding banquet, so that they

may open the door for him as soon as he comes and knocks. ^37Blessed are those slaves whom the master finds alert when he comes; truly I tell you, he will fasten his belt and have them sit down to eat, and he will come and serve them. ^38If he comes during the middle of the night, or near dawn, and finds them so, blessed are those slaves. ^39"But know this: if the owner of the house had known at what hour the thief was coming, he would not have let his house be broken into. ^40You also must be ready, for the Son of Man is coming at an unexpected hour."

^41Peter said, "Lord, are you telling this parable for us or for everyone?" ^42And the Lord said, "Who then is the faithful and prudent manager whom his master will put in charge of his slaves, to give them their allowance of food at the proper time? ^43Blessed is that slave whom his master will find at work when he arrives. ^44Truly I tell you, he will put that one in charge of all his possessions. ^45But if that slave says to himself, 'My master is delayed in coming,' and if he begins to beat the other slaves, men and women, and to eat and drink and get drunk, ^46the master of that slave will come on a day when he does not expect him and at an hour that he does not know, and will cut him in pieces, and put him with the unfaithful. ^47That slave who knew what his master wanted, but did not prepare himself or do what was wanted, will receive a severe beating. ^48But the one who did not know and did what deserved a beating will receive a light beating. From everyone to whom much has been given, much will be required; and from the one to whom much has been entrusted, even more will be demanded. ^49"I came to bring fire to the earth, and how I wish it were already kindled! ^50I have a baptism with which to be baptized, and what stress I am under until it is completed! ⁵¹Do you think that I have come to bring peace to the earth? No, I tell you, but rather division! ⁵²From now on five in one household will be divided, three against two and two against three; ⁵³they will be divided: father against son and son against father, mother against daughter and daughter against mother, mother-in-law against her daughter-in-law and daughter-in-law against mother-in-law."

⁵⁴He also said to the crowds, "When you see a cloud rising in the west, you immediately say, 'It is going to rain'; and so it happens. ⁵⁵And when you see the south wind blowing, you say, 'There will be scorching heat'; and it happens. ⁵⁶You hypocrites! You know how to interpret the appearance of earth and sky, but why do you not know how to interpret the present time? ⁵⁷"And why do you not judge for yourselves what is right? ⁵⁸Thus, when you go with your accuser before a magistrate, on the way make an effort to settle the case, or you may be dragged before the judge, and the judge hand you over to the officer, and the officer throw you in prison. ⁵⁹I tell you, you will never get out until you have paid the very last penny."

# Reflection

After the killing of Michael Brown, Alexis Templeton helped found Millennial Activists United, a key group leading the Ferguson protests. Alexis had neither time nor patience for the clergy or the Church. And she had no problem telling us.

"You all have been sitting in your churches, and we've been out here dying. Now you want to come out and pray and talk to us about Jesus and stuff? You want to be with us? You come and have our backs and face the tear gas and the rubber bullets."

In America, we too quickly substitute be nice and keep the peace for the gospel. Jesus calls us up short in this passage. Jesus attacks the heart of our materialist, consumerist culture. Jesus tells us to watch for him, and that from those to whom much has been given, much is demanded. Jesus promises us it will cause deep division in our most dear relationships when we follow him.

Alexis' call to the Church is Jesus' call. Will we build up treasure on earth—worry about our funders, our reputation? Or will we cast our lot with those who have no earthly treasure and can help us gain none? Will we join Alexis in the street, knowing that it will put us on one side of a conflict, pitting us against friends, family, and those we hold dear? Knowing that from those to whom much has been entrusted, even more will be demanded?

**The Very Rev. Mike Kinman**
**Dean of Christ Church Cathedral**
**St. Louis, Missouri**

## Questions _____

What do you most fear losing? Security? Respect? Safety? Peace? Control?

What are you tempted to choose instead of the risky call of Christ? Who is Alexis and where is "the street" where you are?

Where is Jesus calling you out of your church to stand with Jesus?

## Prayer _____

God, awaken in your Church a longing for your realm of justice, peace, and love, and give each and all of us the passion and courage to risk all to bring it into being. In the name of Jesus, who gave all for the love of the world. *Amen.*

## Luke 13:1-21

13 At that very time there were some present who told him about the Galileans whose blood Pilate had mingled with their sacrifices. ²He asked them, "Do you think that because these Galileans suffered in this way they were worse sinners than all other Galileans? ³No, I tell you; but unless you repent, you will all perish as they did. ⁴Or those eighteen who were killed when the tower of Siloam fell on them—do you think that they were worse offenders than all the others living in Jerusalem? ⁵No, I tell you; but unless you repent, you will all perish just as they did."

⁶Then he told this parable: "A man had a fig tree planted in his vineyard; and he came looking for fruit on it and found none. ⁷So he said to the gardener, 'See here! For three years I have come looking for fruit on this fig tree, and still I find none. Cut it down! Why should it be wasting the soil?' ⁸He replied, 'Sir, let it alone for one more year, until I dig around it and put manure on it. ⁹If it bears fruit next year, well and good; but if not, you can cut it down.'"

¹⁰Now he was teaching in one of the synagogues on the sabbath. ¹¹And just then there appeared a woman with a spirit that had crippled her for eighteen years. She was bent over and was quite unable to stand up straight. ¹²When Jesus saw her, he called her over and said, "Woman, you are set free from your ailment." ¹³When he laid his hands on her, immediately she stood up straight and began praising God. ¹⁴But the leader of the synagogue, indignant because Jesus had cured on the sabbath,

kept saying to the crowd, "There are six days on which work ought to be done; come on those days and be cured, and not on the sabbath day." <sup>15</sup>But the Lord answered him and said, "You hypocrites! Does not each of you on the sabbath untie his ox or his donkey from the manger, and lead it away to give it water? <sup>16</sup>And ought not this woman, a daughter of Abraham whom Satan bound for eighteen long years, be set free from this bondage on the sabbath day?" <sup>17</sup>When he said this, all his opponents were put to shame; and the entire crowd was rejoicing at all the wonderful things that he was doing.

<sup>18</sup>He said therefore, "What is the kingdom of God like? And to what should I compare it? <sup>19</sup>It is like a mustard seed that someone took and sowed in the garden; it grew and became a tree, and the birds of the air made nests in its branches." <sup>20</sup>And again he said, "To what should I compare the kingdom of God? <sup>21</sup>It is like yeast that a woman took and mixed in with three measures of flour until all of it was leavened."

# Reflection

The best mission statement ever written is Canterbury Cathedral's. It's four words: "to show people Jesus."

We could save the Church a lot of time in process and consultants if we would all just adopt that mission statement. We exist to show people Jesus. We will do it at every opportunity. We will do it in ways large and small.

The Jesus we meet in this passage knows that love cannot be constrained. It cannot be constrained by infirmity; it cannot be constrained by rules and conventions; it cannot be constrained by size or stature.

The Jesus we meet in this passage has a sense of immediacy. God's glory, God's love must be made known. It cannot wait. There can be no excuses.

If we do not show people Jesus, then the Church is as much a waste of the soil as the barren fig tree—and we deserve the same fate. If we are worried more about following the rules of respectable society than bringing healing to those in need, then we should sell all we have and give it to someone who is more rightly focused. If we are not out in our communities showing the love of God in Jesus Christ with reckless abandon, then we should make way for someone who will.

We exist to show people Jesus. Right here. Right now. No matter what rational reasons we might give to the contrary. No matter what others might say, we exist to show people Jesus.

**The Very Rev. Mike Kinman**
**Dean of Christ Church Cathedral**
**St. Louis, Missouri**

## Questions _____

How do you and your faith community show Jesus to the world? If your church was given one year to show Jesus to the world in powerful ways, what would you do differently? Why aren't you doing it now?

## Prayer _____

Unbind us, God, from the fears that hold us tightly. Unbind us from the conviction that we must confine your love to the bonds of respectability. Set us free to believe your love for ourselves and to spread your love to the ends of the earth. *Amen.*

## Luke 13:22-35

²²Jesus went through one town and village after another, teaching as he made his way to Jerusalem.

²³Someone asked him, "Lord, will only a few be saved?" He said to them, ²⁴"Strive to enter through the narrow door; for many, I tell you, will try to enter and will not be able. ²⁵When once the owner of the house has got up and shut the door, and you begin to stand outside and to knock at the door, saying, 'Lord, open to us,' then in reply he will say to you, 'I do not know where you come from.' ²⁶Then you will begin to say, 'We ate and drank with you, and you taught in our streets.' ²⁷But he will say, 'I do not know where you come from; go away from me, all you evildoers!' ²⁸There will be weeping and gnashing of teeth when you see Abraham and Isaac and Jacob and all the prophets in the kingdom of God, and you yourselves thrown out. ²⁹Then people will come from east and west, from north and south, and will eat in the kingdom of God. ³⁰Indeed, some are last who will be first, and some are first who will be last."

³¹At that very hour some Pharisees came and said to him, "Get away from here, for Herod wants to kill you." ³²He said to them, "Go and tell that fox for me, 'Listen, I am casting out demons and performing cures today and tomorrow, and on the third day I finish my work. ³³Yet today, tomorrow, and the next day I must be on my way, because it is impossible for a prophet to be killed outside of Jerusalem.' ³⁴Jerusalem, Jerusalem, the city that kills the

prophets and stones those who are sent to it! How often have I desired to gather your children together as a hen gathers her brood under her wings, and you were not willing! ³⁵See, your house is left to you. And I tell you, you will not see me until the time comes when you say, 'Blessed is the one who comes in the name of the Lord.'"

# Reflection

"Everybody wants to go to heaven," Kenny Chesney asserts in a well-known country song, "but nobody wants to go now." As he sits in church, he hears the preacher ask, "'Don't you wanna hear him call your name/When you're standin' at the pearly gates?'/ I told the preacher, 'Yes I do'/But I hope they don't call today./I ain't ready.'"

We are a society and culture of the here and now. Yet we also like to be in control. We "ain't ready" to think about eternal life, and too often when we do, we add up our own good deeds, measure them against the shortcomings we see in others, and rather like our chances. If we must think about what happens when our earthly life ends, we figure that, if we eat and drink with Jesus on Sunday mornings and otherwise conform to what we think this world expects of us, things will turn out just fine.

Jesus turns this thinking on its head. He speaks of the narrow door through which those who hope to be saved must pass. He, not the authorities who claim to be custodians of the law or those who seek to model conventional wisdom, is the doorkeeper. And so "some are last who will be first, and some are first who will be last."

Jesus does not answer the question he is asked: "Lord, will only a few be saved?" He cares little about numbers. Rather he urges us to strive to enter the narrow door or, as Paul writes to the Romans, to "discern what is the will of God—what is good and acceptable and perfect" (Romans 12:2). Jesus is in fact the door—"the way, the truth, and the life" (John 14:6). In humble submission to him, and in thanksgiving for his atoning death, we need not fear Herod or Jerusalem. We will be ready.

**John McCardell**
**Vice-Chancellor and President of the University of the South**
**Sewanee, Tennessee**

## Questions

How might you strive to pass through the narrow door?

What is keeping you from being ready?

## Prayer

Open our eyes, O Lord, to the never-failing presence of your Son. Help us to strive faithfully through the clouds of uncertainty and conformity to things of this world, to discern that which is pleasing in your sight, through Christ our Lord. *Amen.*

## Luke 14:1-24

14 On one occasion when Jesus was going to the house of a leader of the Pharisees to eat a meal on the sabbath, they were watching him closely. [2]Just then, in front of him, there was a man who had dropsy. [3]And Jesus asked the lawyers and Pharisees, "Is it lawful to cure people on the sabbath, or not?" [4]But they were silent. So Jesus took him and healed him, and sent him away. [5]Then he said to them, "If one of you has a child or an ox that has fallen into a well, will you not immediately pull it out on a sabbath day?" [6]And they could not reply to this.

[7]When he noticed how the guests chose the places of honor, he told them a parable. [8]"When you are invited by someone to a wedding banquet, do not sit down at the place of honor, in case someone more distinguished than you has been invited by your host; [9]and the host who invited both of you may come and say to you, 'Give this person your place,' and then in disgrace you would start to take the lowest place. [10]But when you are invited, go and sit down at the lowest place, so that when your host comes, he may say to you, 'Friend, move up higher'; then you will be honored in the presence of all who sit at the table with you. [11]For all who exalt themselves will be humbled, and those who humble themselves will be exalted." [12]He said also to the one who had invited him, "When you give a luncheon or a dinner, do not invite your friends or your brothers or your relatives or rich neighbors, in case they may invite you in

return, and you would be repaid. [13]But when you give a banquet, invite the poor, the crippled, the lame, and the blind. [14]And you will be blessed, because they cannot repay you, for you will be repaid at the resurrection of the righteous."

[15]One of the dinner guests, on hearing this, said to him, "Blessed is anyone who will eat bread in the kingdom of God!" [16]Then Jesus said to him, "Someone gave a great dinner and invited many. [17]At the time for the dinner he sent his slave to say to those who had been invited, 'Come; for everything is ready now.' [18]But they all alike began to make excuses. The first said to him, 'I have bought a piece of land, and I must go out and see it; please accept my regrets.' [19]Another said, 'I have bought five yoke of oxen, and I am going to try them out; please accept my regrets.' [20]Another said, 'I have just been married, and therefore I cannot come.' [21]So the slave returned and reported this to his master. Then the owner of the house became angry and said to his slave, 'Go out at once into the streets and lanes of the town and bring in the poor, the crippled, the blind, and the lame.' [22]And the slave said, 'Sir, what you ordered has been done, and there is still room.' [23]Then the master said to the slave, 'Go out into the roads and lanes, and compel people to come in, so that my house may be filled. [24]For I tell you, none of those who were invited will taste my dinner.'"

# Reflection

Most of us have seen, perhaps multiple times, the movie *The Sound of Music*. The stage version, however, includes a song that did not make it into the film. Its title is "No Way to Stop It," and it includes these words: "So every star and every whirling planet, And every constellation in the sky, Revolves around the center of the universe, That lovely thing called I."

It is hard not to be self-referential. It is challenging to see things through eyes other than our own. It is confounding when the judgments of others differ from ours. And yet from the beginning of human history, we have always tried, and always failed, to be like God.

This passage is not an etiquette lesson. Nor is it about winning friends and influencing people. Rather, it is about humility, and about doubting a little of our own infallibility. In performing an act of healing on the Sabbath, Jesus scandalizes those who uphold the sacred law. In observing their unseemly vying for the most prestigious places at table, he offers an alternative to their status-conscious self-promotion.

Let repentance and humility, born of kind hearts, replace rigid minds and sharp elbows, Jesus says. Heal the sick. Take the humblest seat. Invite those to your meal who cannot possibly repay you. Repayment will come—in the fullness of time, on the day of resurrection—when he who humbled himself to death on a cross, for us and for our sins, invites the faithful to the heavenly banquet.

**John McCardell**
**Vice-Chancellor and President of the University of the South**
**Sewanee, Tennessee**

## Question

Can you think of moments in your life when self-denial proved to be a blessing?

## Prayer

Lord, teach us to deny ourselves and to follow you. Help us to see status and wealth as neither a measure of who we are nor an impediment to what we seek to become. Give us hearts and minds to love and serve our neighbors as ourselves. In Christ's name we pray. *Amen.*

## Luke 14:25-35

<sup>25</sup>Now large crowds were traveling with him; and he turned and said to them, <sup>26</sup>"Whoever comes to me and does not hate father and mother, wife and children, brothers and sisters, yes, and even life itself, cannot be my disciple. <sup>27</sup>Whoever does not carry the cross and follow me cannot be my disciple. <sup>28</sup>For which of you, intending to build a tower, does not first sit down and estimate the cost, to see whether he has enough to complete it? <sup>29</sup>Otherwise, when he has laid a foundation and is not able to finish, all who see it will begin to ridicule him, <sup>30</sup>saying, 'This fellow began to build and was not able to finish.' <sup>31</sup>Or what king, going out to wage war against another king, will not sit down first and consider whether he is able with ten thousand to oppose the one who comes against him with twenty thousand? <sup>32</sup>If he cannot, then, while the other is still far away, he sends a delegation and asks for the terms of peace. <sup>33</sup>So therefore, none of you can become my disciple if you do not give up all your possessions. <sup>34</sup>"Salt is good; but if salt has lost its taste, how can its saltiness be restored? <sup>35</sup>It is fit neither for the soil nor for the manure pile; they throw it away. Let anyone with ears to hear listen!"

# Reflection

In this text, Jesus issues the challenging and life-transforming statement: "Take up your cross and follow me."

One way of looking at this is to see it as a sadistic kind of demand—to go out and get a cross and die Christ's kind of death. And yet people like Saint Francis of Assisi followed Christ and died peacefully in bed. The challenge of the invitation is not that we go out and seek meaningless suffering but that we offer ourselves in love for and with others.

Another way of seeing this cross-talk is to see it as frivolous. For years golfers would talk about Tiger Woods as their "cross to bear." Depending on your college and sport of choice, many people talk about the rival coach and team as a cross.

The gospel proclaims that our lives are to be shaped by cross-bearing, but most of the time we merely resort to cross-wearing.

Singer Madonna was speaking recently on a talk show. The interviewer noticed her diamond-studded cross around her neck. She declared: "I may not wear much else, but I always wear my cross."

At Tiffany's jewelry store in London, a customer was looking for a cross for his mate. The store clerk asked: "Do you want a plain one or one with the little man on it?"

"Take up your cross and follow me" is an invitation that is neither sadistic nor frivolous. Jesus asks us to pick up our crosses, not his, and to carry them to the place of resolution, restoration, and resurrection. Jesus' crucifixion could have been merely one more obscenity committed in the name of religion, but Jesus' obedience, self-offering, and love were too powerful to die on a cross, and in his Resurrection he sets us free to love and serve in his name.

**The Rev. Robert S. Dannals**
**Rector of Saint Michael and All Angels Church**
**Dallas, Texas**

## Questions _____

The noted theologian Dietrich Bonhoeffer asked decades ago, "Who is Jesus Christ for us today?" How is this timeless question connected with Jesus' statement to take up your cross and follow him?

What are some of the crosses you are asked to bear? Who and what enables and strengthens you to bear them?

How does Jesus' Resurrection bring you hope in the midst of your "crosses"?

## Prayer _____

Gracious God, who offers compassionate love in the cross of Christ, let the cry of those who suffer come to you, that they may find in your cross and Resurrection the mercy and strength to bear their burdens. Give us, we pray, the love to serve those who face the crosses of our day, for the sake of him who suffered for us, your Son Jesus Christ our Lord. *Amen.*

## Luke 15:1-10

**15** Now all the tax collectors and sinners were coming near to listen to him. ²And the Pharisees and the scribes were grumbling and saying, "This fellow welcomes sinners and eats with them." ³So he told them this parable: ⁴"Which one of you, having a hundred sheep and losing one of them, does not leave the ninety-nine in the wilderness and go after the one that is lost until he finds it? ⁵When he has found it, he lays it on his shoulders and rejoices. ⁶And when he comes home, he calls together his friends and neighbors, saying to them, 'Rejoice with me, for I have found my sheep that was lost.' ⁷Just so, I tell you, there will be more joy in heaven over one sinner who repents than over ninety-nine righteous persons who need no repentance. ⁸"Or what woman having ten silver coins, if she loses one of them, does not light a lamp, sweep the house, and search carefully until she finds it? ⁹When she has found it, she calls together her friends and neighbors, saying, 'Rejoice with me, for I have found the coin that I had lost.' ¹⁰Just so, I tell you, there is joy in the presence of the angels of God over one sinner who repents."

# Reflection

It is often said that you can tell what a person is like by the company that she or he keeps. You remember the old saying, "Birds of a feather flock together." But it's not the whole truth! Jesus was a friend of sinners not because he easily excused unjust behavior, but because he wanted to exercise loving influence.

This text reminds us that when we join those who are sinners, we lose our way and get separated from our moorings. Sometimes we want to object to this analysis, denying that we are part of the condition. But in our heart of hearts we know better.

So, why is it that so many people feel lost? Alienated? In an ocean of social media that is supposed to keep us connected, there is an epidemic of isolation and loneliness.

It seems to me that the challenge is based on two extremes: It's not my fault; don't count on me and it's all my fault; I'll fix it.

I used to wonder why Jesus was so hard on the Pharisees, because in their society they were considered the good guys. I now realize that Jesus saw in them (and us) the problems of both self-deprecation and its opposite, self-righteousness, as the most deadly spiritual conditions that one could have.

In the face of this, Jesus extends radical hospitality and grace. He is the lover of the lost, friend of the damaged, host of the masses. His welcome and meal fellowship includes the woman with a blood disease, a man plagued by demons, sisters caught in sibling rivalry— and you and me, and the people we don't especially like.

**The Rev. Robert S. Dannals**
**Rector of Saint Michael and All Angels Church**
**Dallas, Texas**

## Questions

Insofar as moral codes are used as stepping stones to independence from God, how do you suppose God's radical grace, welcoming all comers, squares with God's intentions that we behave morally, that we follow the rules?

Who are the outcasts of society and/or of your community?

What can you do to enhance their inclusion, following the example of Jesus?

## Prayer

Gracious God, whose compassionate Son on many occasions welcomed outcasts, ate with sinners, and befriended the loveless, mercifully grant that we may receive thankfully the table fellowship of Jesus, who in the holy mysteries of the Eucharist gives us a pledge of God's presence and an example to follow in our day; and who now lives and reigns with you and the Holy Spirit, one God, for ever and ever. *Amen.*

## Luke 15:11-32

[11]Then Jesus said, "There was a man who had two sons. [12]The younger of them said to his father, 'Father, give me the share of the property that will belong to me.' So he divided his property between them. [13]A few days later the younger son gathered all he had and traveled to a distant country, and there he squandered his property in dissolute living. [14]When he had spent everything, a severe famine took place throughout that country, and he began to be in need. [15]So he went and hired himself out to one of the citizens of that country, who sent him to his fields to feed the pigs. [16]He would gladly have filled himself with the pods that the pigs were eating; and no one gave him anything. [17]But when he came to himself he said, 'How many of my father's hired hands have bread enough and to spare, but here I am dying of hunger! [18]I will get up and go to my father, and I will say to him, "Father, I have sinned against heaven and before you; [19]I am no longer worthy to be called your son; treat me like one of your hired hands."' [20]So he set off and went to his father. But while he was still far off, his father saw him and was filled with compassion; he ran and put his arms around him and kissed him. [21]Then the son said to him, 'Father, I have sinned against heaven and before you; I am no longer worthy to be called your son.' [22]But the father said to his slaves, 'Quickly, bring out a robe—the best one—and put it on him; put a ring on his finger and sandals on his feet. [23]And get the fatted calf and kill it, and let us eat and celebrate; [24]for this son of mine was dead and is alive again; he was lost and is found!' And they

began to celebrate. ²⁵"Now his elder son was in the field; and when he came and approached the house, he heard music and dancing. ²⁶He called one of the slaves and asked what was going on. ²⁷He replied, 'Your brother has come, and your father has killed the fatted calf, because he has got him back safe and sound.' ²⁸Then he became angry and refused to go in. His father came out and began to plead with him. ²⁹But he answered his father, 'Listen! For all these years I have been working like a slave for you, and I have never disobeyed your command; yet you have never given me even a young goat so that I might celebrate with my friends. ³⁰But when this son of yours came back, who has devoured your property with prostitutes, you killed the fatted calf for him!' ³¹Then the father said to him, 'Son, you are always with me, and all that is mine is yours. ³²But we had to celebrate and rejoice, because this brother of yours was dead and has come to life; he was lost and has been found.'"

# Reflection

This parable follows two others about losing and finding; the prodigal son is really best understood as a lost son who, as the father of the story proclaims with joy, is found in the end.

The coin and the sheep, whose stories precede this one, offer no real picture of what being lost really means—they've just gone missing. But this story explores being lost, and it takes us into some unattractive depths. Some of us may easily dismiss the story of the son as far removed from our own; others will see themselves in it more readily. Being lost, from our perspective, means being far from who and where we are meant to be, and sometimes it's something we do to ourselves—we get ourselves lost, and sometimes we want to stay so, or imagine that going home is too hard.

God, however, treats us not as rebellious or repulsive, but merely as missing, and valued too—worth being sought after in the wilderness, swept out from the dark corner, or welcomed with open arms. We may find the idea of the journey home too hard even to imagine, but God does not, and it is God who seeks and who welcomes. This parable also gives us an image of what it means to be found—not shamed or exposed but loved and welcomed unconditionally.

**Andrew B. McGowan**
**Dean of the Berkeley Divinity School at Yale**
**New Haven, Connecticut**

*A Journey with Luke*

## Questions_____

Are you lost, or were you once?

Have you acknowledged that God's seeking is what brought you home, or are you still on the way?

## Prayer _____

God who seeks and finds, when we were still far off, you met us and brought us home. May we feast joyfully with you and share your joy generously with others whom you seek and who seek you; through Jesus Christ our Lord. *Amen.*

## Luke 16:1-18

16 Then Jesus said to the disciples, "There was a rich man who had a manager, and charges were brought to him that this man was squandering his property. ²So he summoned him and said to him, 'What is this that I hear about you? Give me an accounting of your management, because you cannot be my manager any longer.' ³Then the manager said to himself, 'What will I do, now that my master is taking the position away from me? I am not strong enough to dig, and I am ashamed to beg. ⁴I have decided what to do so that, when I am dismissed as manager, people may welcome me into their homes.' ⁵So, summoning his master's debtors one by one, he asked the first, 'How much do you owe my master?' ⁶He answered, 'A hundred jugs of olive oil.' He said to him, 'Take your bill, sit down quickly, and make it fifty.' ⁷Then he asked another, 'And how much do you owe?' He replied, 'A hundred containers of wheat.' He said to him, 'Take your bill and make it eighty.' ⁸And his master commended the dishonest manager because he had acted shrewdly; for the children of this age are more shrewd in dealing with their own generation than are the children of light. ⁹And I tell you, make friends for yourselves by means of dishonest wealth so that when it is gone, they may welcome you into the eternal homes. ¹⁰"Whoever is faithful in a very little is faithful also in much; and whoever is dishonest in a very little is dishonest also in much. ¹¹If then you have not been faithful with the dishonest wealth, who will entrust to you the true riches? ¹²And if

you have not been faithful with what belongs to another, who will give you what is your own? [13]No slave can serve two masters; for a slave will either hate the one and love the other, or be devoted to the one and despise the other. You cannot serve God and wealth." [14]The Pharisees, who were lovers of money, heard all this, and they ridiculed him. [15]So he said to them, "You are those who justify yourselves in the sight of others; but God knows your hearts; for what is prized by human beings is an abomination in the sight of God. [16]"The law and the prophets were in effect until John came; since then the good news of the kingdom of God is proclaimed, and everyone tries to enter it by force. [17]But it is easier for heaven and earth to pass away, than for one stroke of a letter in the law to be dropped. [18]"Anyone who divorces his wife and marries another commits adultery, and whoever marries a woman divorced from her husband commits adultery.

# Reflection

Luke's Gospel consistently shows interest in issues of wealth and poverty, presenting many stories and sayings of Jesus that urge charitable and just behavior. This seems to imply that many of its readers and hearers might exercise economic power and face important choices that could affect their lives and the lives of others. The parable of the unjust manager or steward would hardly make sense without a context where decisions like these—cutting one's losses in one area for the sake of gains in another—were conceivable.

There seem to be two morals to this story. The first is fairly literal and has to do with actual money: "make friends for yourselves by means of dishonest wealth." Generosity and the connections it can bring are desirable but not for their own sake—these are urged because thus "they may welcome you into the eternal homes." Note however that this is "dishonest wealth," emphasizing the ultimate worthlessness of material goods as well as the importance of what else there is to gain.

Jesus goes on to make the contrast even sharper: "you cannot serve God and wealth." First then, despite the label "unjust" applied to the manager, we are called to act justly and charitably. Secondly however, and just as importantly, the things we use in the present to benefit ourselves and others must be put in perspective. God alone is worth serving.

**Andrew B. McGowan**
**Dean of the Berkeley Divinity School at Yale**
**New Haven, Connecticut**

## Questions

How is faith involved in your daily financial decisions?

Is it tempting to treat God as one creditor to be paid among others, rather than as the source and end of all real wealth?

## Prayer

God of all creation, through your goodness we have all that sustains our lives. Accept the offering of all that we have and use it and us for your glory; through Jesus Christ our Lord. *Amen.*

## Luke 16:19-31

[19]"There was a rich man who was dressed in purple and fine linen and who feasted sumptuously every day. [20]And at his gate lay a poor man named Lazarus, covered with sores, [21]who longed to satisfy his hunger with what fell from the rich man's table; even the dogs would come and lick his sores. [22]The poor man died and was carried away by the angels to be with Abraham. The rich man also died and was buried. [23]In Hades, where he was being tormented, he looked up and saw Abraham far away with Lazarus by his side. [24]He called out, 'Father Abraham, have mercy on me, and send Lazarus to dip the tip of his finger in water and cool my tongue; for I am in agony in these flames.' [25]But Abraham said, 'Child, remember that during your lifetime you received your good things, and Lazarus in like manner evil things; but now he is comforted here, and you are in agony. [26]Besides all this, between you and us a great chasm has been fixed, so that those who might want to pass from here to you cannot do so, and no one can cross from there to us.' [27]He said, 'Then, father, I beg you to send him to my father's house—[28]for I have five brothers—that he may warn them, so that they will not also come into this place of torment.' [29]Abraham replied, 'They have Moses and the prophets; they should listen to them.' [30]He said, 'No, father Abraham; but if someone goes to them from the dead, they will repent.' [31]He said to him, 'If they do not listen to Moses and the prophets, neither will they be convinced even if someone rises from the dead.'

# Reflection

This story reminds me of Jacob Marley's ghost in *A Christmas Carol*, who managed to finagle his way back over the chasm to warn his former business partner that he ought to think about mending his ways before it was too late. Although Marley was able to jump-start him on the process of metanoia, Scrooge was finally convinced only after the visitations of a persuasive trinity of specters.

Notice some things about our story from Luke's Jesus: of the two main characters, only Lazarus has a name. The rich dude, for all his excess, is denied that. Yet Mr. No Name, who apparently didn't happen to see or intentionally ignored the poor guy begging just outside his gated household when they were both still alive, now knows and calls Lazarus by name. Even with this bit of recognition, he still doesn't really see him. He never talks to Lazarus, ignores him as if Lazarus weren't there. And he still treats him like a lackey, first to fetch some water for him and then to scare his brothers into mending their ways.

Things seem grim for Mr. No Name. But this is a parable, and Jesus' parables are nearly always left open. And Hades isn't hell as we latter-day believers understand it. This isn't the end for the rich dude. He's in what his contemporaries understand to be a sort of waiting room before final judgment. Although he still hasn't learned to respect the dignity of this fellow human being, he begins to show concern for others rather than solely for himself; there's a tiny crack in his self-absorption. In the words of Leonard Cohen's song *Anthem*, "There is a crack in everything, that's how the light gets in."

**Vicki Garvey**
**Associate for Lifelong Christian Formation**
**for the Diocese of Chicago**
**Chicago, Illinois**

## Question _____

Who are we ignoring as if they weren't there?

What's the source of our discomfort, and how might we train ourselves to pay attention?

## Prayer _____

Our God, you continue to give us second and third and infinite chances, and for your patience and trust in us, we thank you. Please help us to be as lavish in our generosity to others, that we may be the people of God you call us to be. *Amen.*

## Luke 17:1-10

17 Jesus said to his disciples, "Occasions for stumbling are bound to come, but woe to anyone by whom they come! ²It would be better for you if a millstone were hung around your neck and you were thrown into the sea than for you to cause one of these little ones to stumble. ³Be on your guard! If another disciple sins, you must rebuke the offender, and if there is repentance, you must forgive. ⁴And if the same person sins against you seven times a day, and turns back to you seven times and says, 'I repent,' you must forgive." ⁵The apostles said to the Lord, "Increase our faith!" ⁶The Lord replied, "If you had faith the size of a mustard seed, you could say to this mulberry tree, 'Be uprooted and planted in the sea,' and it would obey you. ⁷"Who among you would say to your slave who has just come in from plowing or tending sheep in the field, 'Come here at once and take your place at the table'? ⁸Would you not rather say to him, 'Prepare supper for me, put on your apron and serve me while I eat and drink; later you may eat and drink'? ⁹Do you thank the slave for doing what was commanded? ¹⁰So you also, when you have done all that you were ordered to do, say, 'We are worthless slaves; we have done only what we ought to have done!'"

# Reflection

Several years ago, I facilitated a Bible study focused on Luke. In this group were men who had served this country proudly in World War II. They saw themselves as individuals who had pulled themselves up by their bootstraps and thought everybody else ought to do the same. They had little patience with those they felt hadn't pay their dues; they were by-the-book sorts who believed in rules and who lived by that creed. They were also kind and generous men who took their faith seriously—except, they admitted to me, when they had difficulties with it.

We had been meeting for nearly two years when this portion of the gospel came up. By this time I had finally convinced them that good Bible study was not about my telling them arcane tidbits about a Greek verb or about the Roman economy in the first century but about the Bible reaching them in their situations in the twenty-first. It happened that this particular week we met on the day after the execution of Timothy McVeigh, one of the architects of the bombing of the Oklahoma City federal building. By their customary way of thinking, McVeigh deserved what he got. One of the men read this text aloud. The silence between his proclamation and their first comment was longer than usual. Finally, one asked me, "Do you think this business of forgiving seven times has anything to do with what happened yesterday?" I countered, "What do you think?" One of the men responded, eyes to heaven, "Please increase our faith." Then we had a long conversation about capital punishment and forgiveness and the sometimes hard things our faith asks of us.

**Vicki Garvey**
**Associate for Lifelong Christian Formation**
**for the Diocese of Chicago**
**Chicago, Illinois**

## Questions_____

Do you ever find yourself wanting to ignore something in the Bible, something that Jesus is advocating or even commanding?

When this happens, what do you do about it?

## Prayer _____

Our God, your thoughts aren't ours and sometimes your ways seem too demanding for us. Please help us to be larger in our generosity of spirit, to welcome others as you welcome each of us, especially when those others are difficult for us to understand or love. *Amen.*

## Luke 17:11-37

[11]On the way to Jerusalem Jesus was going through the region between Samaria and Galilee. [12]As he entered a village, ten lepers approached him. Keeping their distance, [13]they called out, saying, "Jesus, Master, have mercy on us!" [14]When he saw them, he said to them, "Go and show yourselves to the priests." And as they went, they were made clean. [15]Then one of them, when he saw that he was healed, turned back, praising God with a loud voice. [16]He prostrated himself at Jesus' feet and thanked him. And he was a Samaritan. [17]Then Jesus asked, "Were not ten made clean? But the other nine, where are they? [18]Was none of them found to return and give praise to God except this foreigner?" [19]Then he said to him, "Get up and go on your way; your faith has made you well."

[20]Once Jesus was asked by the Pharisees when the kingdom of God was coming, and he answered, "The kingdom of God is not coming with things that can be observed; [21]nor will they say, 'Look, here it is!' or 'There it is!' For, in fact, the kingdom of God is among you." [22]Then he said to the disciples, "The days are coming when you will long to see one of the days of the Son of Man, and you will not see it. [23]They will say to you, 'Look there!' or 'Look here!' Do not go, do not set off in pursuit. [24]For as the lightning flashes and lights up the sky from one side to the other, so will the Son of Man be in his day. [25]But first he must endure much suffering and be rejected by this generation. [26]Just as it was in the days of Noah, so too it will be in the days of the Son of Man. [27]They were eating and drinking, and

marrying and being given in marriage, until the day Noah entered the ark, and the flood came and destroyed all of them. ²⁸Likewise, just as it was in the days of Lot: they were eating and drinking, buying and selling, planting and building, ²⁹but on the day that Lot left Sodom, it rained fire and sulfur from heaven and destroyed all of them ³⁰—it will be like that on the day that the Son of Man is revealed. ³¹On that day, anyone on the housetop who has belongings in the house must not come down to take them away; and likewise anyone in the field must not turn back. ³²Remember Lot's wife. ³³Those who try to make their life secure will lose it, but those who lose their life will keep it. ³⁴I tell you, on that night there will be two in one bed; one will be taken and the other left. ³⁵There will be two women grinding meal together; one will be taken and the other left." ³⁷Then they asked him, "Where, Lord?" He said to them, "Where the corpse is, there the vultures will gather."

# Reflection

The time horizon of Jesus' teaching and ministry stretched from the immediate, present moment to the unveiling of God's final revelation. In this passage, he demonstrates his concern with both.

First, he heals ten lepers who present themselves before him. According to the Jewish law, those who thought they were healed had to show themselves to priests in the temple. Jesus instructs them to do so and all are healed. But only one—a Samaritan, the outcast in the group—thinks to turn back and thank Jesus.

Second, Jesus speaks at length about what is to come. This is called an eschatological discourse because it concerns the end (Greek: eschaton) times. Such passages can be difficult to understand. But they remind us that our lives are wrapped up in the much broader story of God's action. Throughout history, people have found such passages to be reasons for hope: God is acting in our midst to bring Creation to consummation. That consummation will be so rich and powerful that it will make our current existence seem a bare shadow, to which we will have no reason to turn back.

Uniting the present moment and the future glory is a short teaching about a topic of central importance: the kingdom of God. When we are following Jesus, the kingdom of God is in our midst as a present reality. But it is also a future reality. We look to its full unveiling in hope and expectation. As Christians, we are called to live with gratitude and hope in the present moment while we also look expectantly toward the future.

The Rev. Jesse Zink
Assistant Chaplain at Emmanuel College
Cambridge, England

## Questions

Jesus said, "The kingdom of God is among you." Where do you see the kingdom of God as a present reality?

Where is the kingdom of God yet to come?

## Prayer

Holy God, guide us into the ways of gratitude and hope that we may be drawn fully into your kingdom. Help us to look expectantly for the signs of your work in this world and keep us watchful and waiting for your future glory. In the name of Christ. *Amen.*

## Luke 18:1-17

18 Then Jesus told them a parable about their need to pray always and not to lose heart. ²He said, "In a certain city there was a judge who neither feared God nor had respect for people. ³In that city there was a widow who kept coming to him and saying, 'Grant me justice against my opponent.' ⁴For a while he refused; but later he said to himself, 'Though I have no fear of God and no respect for anyone, ⁵yet because this widow keeps bothering me, I will grant her justice, so that she may not wear me out by continually coming.'" ⁶And the Lord said, "Listen to what the unjust judge says. ⁷And will not God grant justice to his chosen ones who cry to him day and night? Will he delay long in helping them? ⁸I tell you, he will quickly grant justice to them. And yet, when the Son of Man comes, will he find faith on earth?"

⁹He also told this parable to some who trusted in themselves that they were righteous and regarded others with contempt: ¹⁰"Two men went up to the temple to pray, one a Pharisee and the other a tax collector. ¹¹The Pharisee, standing by himself, was praying thus, 'God, I thank you that I am not like other people: thieves, rogues, adulterers, or even like this tax collector. ¹²I fast twice a week; I give a tenth of all my income.' ¹³But the tax collector, standing far off, would not even look up to heaven, but was beating his breast and saying, 'God, be merciful to me, a sinner!' ¹⁴I tell you, this man went down to his home justified rather than the other; for all who exalt themselves will be humbled, but

all who humble themselves will be exalted."

[15]People were bringing even infants to him that he might touch them; and when the disciples saw it, they sternly ordered them not to do it. [16]But Jesus called for them and said, "Let the little children come to me, and do not stop them; for it is to such as these that the kingdom of God belongs. [17]Truly I tell you, whoever does not receive the kingdom of God as a little child will never enter it."

# Reflection

In Luke's Gospel, Jesus has a particular concern with prayer. Time and again, we read that at significant moments—his baptism, choosing disciples, the Transfiguration—Jesus was praying. In this passage, Jesus tells his followers why prayer is so important.

The first story compares prayer to an elderly woman who continually berates a judge until he gives her justice. If prayer to our merciful God is like this, it means prayer is best seen not as a one-off action but as a pattern of living and being in relationship with God. The second story compares the prayers of an upright Pharisee and a self-abased tax collector. God desires the prayers not of the righteous but of those who are humbly aware of their shortcomings. In one of his final moments of prayer, Jesus models these virtues. At Gethsemane before his arrest, he is the picture of humility before God: "yet not my will but yours be done."

Jesus' teachings about prayer come in the middle of several teachings about the kingdom of God. This is not a mistake: for Jesus, prayer is how the community of his followers will realize the kingdom of God in their midst. The values and virtues of the kingdom are brought about by our humble and frequent prayers that create and sustain a relationship with our merciful God.

Prayer can oftentimes be seen as a transactional relationship between a Christian and God. Instead, Jesus is reminding us that prayer is how we are drawn deeper into the life of our Triune God and into God's plan for our world.

**The Rev. Jesse Zink**
**Assistant Chaplain at Emmanuel College**
**Cambridge, England**

*A Journey with Luke*

## Questions

How do you pray?

What habits and practices are most useful to your prayer life?

How can your prayer life be connected to the kingdom of God?

## Prayer

Lord Jesus, you taught us to pray for the coming of your kingdom. Build in us faithful and honest patterns of prayer that draw us deeper into your life and love. Then send us out into your world to teach others to pray as you have taught us. In your name we pray. *Amen.*

## Luke 18:18-43

¹⁸A certain ruler asked him, "Good Teacher, what must I do to inherit eternal life?" ¹⁹Jesus said to him, "Why do you call me good? No one is good but God alone. ²⁰You know the commandments: 'You shall not commit adultery; You shall not murder; You shall not steal; You shall not bear false witness; Honor your father and mother.'" ²¹He replied, "I have kept all these since my youth." ²²When Jesus heard this, he said to him, "There is still one thing lacking. Sell all that you own and distribute the money to the poor, and you will have treasure in heaven; then come, follow me." ²³But when he heard this, he became sad; for he was very rich. ²⁴Jesus looked at him and said, "How hard it is for those who have wealth to enter the kingdom of God! ²⁵Indeed, it is easier for a camel to go through the eye of a needle than for someone who is rich to enter the kingdom of God." ²⁶Those who heard it said, "Then who can be saved?" ²⁷He replied, "What is impossible for mortals is possible for God." ²⁸Then Peter said, "Look, we have left our homes and followed you." ²⁹And he said to them, "Truly I tell you, there is no one who has left house or wife or brothers or parents or children, for the sake of the kingdom of God, ³⁰who will not get back very much more in this age, and in the age to come eternal life."

³¹Then he took the twelve aside and said to them, "See, we are going up to Jerusalem, and everything that is written about the Son of Man by the prophets will be accomplished. ³²For he will be handed over to the Gentiles; and he will be

mocked and insulted and spat upon. ³³After they have flogged him, they will kill him, and on the third day he will rise again." ³⁴But they understood nothing about all these things; in fact, what he said was hidden from them, and they did not grasp what was said.

³⁵As he approached Jericho, a blind man was sitting by the roadside begging. ³⁶When he heard a crowd going by, he asked what was happening. ³⁷They told him, "Jesus of Nazareth is passing by." ³⁸Then he shouted, "Jesus, Son of David, have mercy on me!" ³⁹Those who were in front sternly ordered him to be quiet; but he shouted even more loudly, "Son of David, have mercy on me!" ⁴⁰Jesus stood still and ordered the man to be brought to him; and when he came near, he asked him, ⁴¹"What do you want me to do for you?" He said, "Lord, let me see again." ⁴²Jesus said to him, "Receive your sight; your faith has saved you." ⁴³Immediately he regained his sight and followed him, glorifying God; and all the people, when they saw it, praised God.

# Reflection

When I was in seminary, the most important lesson I learned did not occur in a classroom, in a field work setting, or being stirred to a new insight by an inspiring sermon. It occurred in my car. One of my professors asked me to pick up noted New Testament scholar Krister Stendahl who was flying in to speak at Virginia Theological Seminary.

What a gift, I thought, to have a precious few moments with one of the Church's best minds. We talked a bit and then I asked him, "What would you tell this young seminarian who has just finished his first year of study?" He thought for a moment and then whispered, "Remember Jesus. Remember Jesus and his Cross. All of our conversation, our jokes, our stories these days are about the Church—not Jesus; remember Jesus." From that day, over two decades ago, until now, when writing letters, journal entries, class notes, I write the date and then under that date, the two words, "Remember Jesus."

These three vignettes from Luke's Gospel are about focusing on Jesus. The rich young ruler has found that both wealth and piety leave him empty. Jesus tells him to give up the one thing that gets in the way of relationship, and follow. Remember Jesus.

Jesus then tells his followers that discipleship means more than being schooled in the ways of God; that ultimately this following will carry their master to a cross and an empty grave. It is not about rules, it is about relationship; it is not about a new religion, it is about God in Christ. Remember Jesus.

Lastly, a blind beggar wants healing. "Lord, I want to see," he says. The blind beggar is given an inner sight to know where to turn for healing—Jesus. The good Lord provides it and the man is healed. Remember Jesus.

Stendahl was right, and still is. It is Jesus who saves us; it is his death and resurrection that transforms us. Jesus is the one who heals us and makes us whole. Remember Jesus.

**The Rev. Russell Levenson Jr.**
**Rector of St. Martin's Church**
**Houston, Texas**

## Questions

What strikes you about the focus of these passages?

Has something, or someone, caused the focus of your discipleship to be other than on Jesus? If so, what can you do to reorient your focus—to remember Jesus?

## Prayer

Almighty God, Where I have strayed, bring me home; When I have turned from you, turn me back; Where I am on the right path, guide me further; When I am following faithfully, take me deeper; Into the grace, and life and love of your child, my Savior, Jesus. *Amen.*

## Luke 19:1-27

19He entered Jericho and was passing through it. ²A man was there named Zacchaeus; he was a chief tax collector and was rich. ³He was trying to see who Jesus was, but on account of the crowd he could not, because he was short in stature. ⁴So he ran ahead and climbed a sycamore tree to see him, because he was going to pass that way. ⁵When Jesus came to the place, he looked up and said to him, "Zacchaeus, hurry and come down; for I must stay at your house today." ⁶So he hurried down and was happy to welcome him. ⁷All who saw it began to grumble and said, "He has gone to be the guest of one who is a sinner." ⁸Zacchaeus stood there and said to the Lord, "Look, half of my possessions, Lord, I will give to the poor; and if I have defrauded anyone of anything, I will pay back four times as much." ⁹Then Jesus said to him, "Today salvation has come to this house, because he too is a son of Abraham. ¹⁰For the Son of Man came to seek out and to save the lost."

¹¹As they were listening to this, he went on to tell a parable, because he was near Jerusalem, and because they supposed that the kingdom of God was to appear immediately. ¹²So he said, "A nobleman went to a distant country to get royal power for himself and then return. ¹³He summoned ten of his slaves, and gave them ten pounds, and said to them, 'Do business with these until I come back.' ¹⁴But the citizens of his country hated him and sent a delegation after him, saying, 'We do not want this man to rule over us.' ¹⁵When he returned, having received royal

power, he ordered these slaves, to whom he had given the money, to be summoned so that he might find out what they had gained by trading. <sup>16</sup>The first came forward and said, 'Lord, your pound has made ten more pounds.' <sup>17</sup>He said to him, 'Well done, good slave! Because you have been trustworthy in a very small thing, take charge of ten cities.' <sup>18</sup>Then the second came, saying, 'Lord, your pound has made five pounds.' <sup>19</sup>He said to him, 'And you, rule over five cities.' <sup>20</sup>Then the other came, saying, 'Lord, here is your pound. I wrapped it up in a piece of cloth, <sup>21</sup>for I was afraid of you, because you are a harsh man; you take what you did not deposit, and reap what you did not sow.' <sup>22</sup>He said to him, 'I will judge you by your own words, you wicked slave! You knew, did you, that I was a harsh man, taking what I did not deposit and reaping what I did not sow? <sup>23</sup>Why then did you not put my money into the bank? Then when I returned, I could have collected it with interest.' <sup>24</sup>He said to the bystanders, 'Take the pound from him and give it to the one who has ten pounds.' <sup>25</sup>(And they said to him, 'Lord, he has ten pounds!') <sup>26</sup>'I tell you, to all those who have, more will be given; but from those who have nothing, even what they have will be taken away. <sup>27</sup>But as for these enemies of mine who did not want me to be king over them—bring them here and slaughter them in my presence.'"

# Reflection

When word reached Elizabeth Tudor that she would be the new reigning monarch upon the death of her sister, Queen Mary, she was heard to say, *"A domino factum est illud, et est mirable in oculis meis!"* The words come from Psalm 118:23: "This is the Lord's doing and it is marvelous in our eyes." Though it was only the beginning, it was also a proclamation that her life yet to come was about living into her vocation as Queen of England.

The two scenes from today's reading remind us that we Christians too have a calling on our lives—to be evangelists and to faithfully use our gifts for the purposes of God's kingdom.

First, we see Jesus reaching out to touch one who earnestly wanted to meet him. Little Zacchaeus, often overlooked (literally) by those around him, was not beyond Jesus' vision. He wanted to see Jesus. Jesus gave him more—a meeting and likely a new beginning for the little man.

Second, the teaching, best known to us as the parable of the talents, is about putting to use what God has entrusted into our care by using the marvelous calling on our lives to serve others.

What both passages remind us is that we are put here to do more than live. We are put here to reach out to others for the sake of Christ. Zacchaeus reminds us we are to be constantly on the lookout for those who want to meet Jesus. And Jesus then reminds us that we are put here for a reason. As it is written in the letter to the Ephesians, "For we are what he has made us, created in Christ Jesus for good works, which God prepared beforehand to be our way of life" (2:10).

This calling on our lives goes not just for monarchs, but for all who follow our Lord. It goes for stay-at-home moms and dads, for garbage collectors and physicians, for pool cleaners and attorneys, for rock stars and CEOs. Serving God and serving others is what we were put on this earth to do—it is our vocation. As theologian Frederick Buechner writes, "The place God calls you to is the place where your deep gladness and the world's hunger meet."

So, ask for eyes to see those who desire to meet Jesus, and then invite them to do just that. And ask for the eyes to see your own talents and then put them to good use by building God's kingdom right where you are. In doing this, surely, your service will be "marvelous" in God's eyes.

**The Rev. Russell Levenson Jr.**
**Rector of St. Martin's Church**
**Houston, Texas**

## Questions_____

Knowing God calls us to invite everyone into a relationship with Jesus, whom might you have overlooked?

How can you better use the talents God has given you to further God's kingdom?

Do you see your work as a job or a vocation? How do you serve others through your work?

## Prayer _____

O God, I seek a love that is already there; I want to know a love that is already present; help me in my frailty and self-centeredness to open my heart to your love. Fill me afresh, so that made whole with that love, I may share it with all you send my way. In the name of God, whose other name is Love. *Amen.*

## Luke 19:28-48

28After he had said this, he went on ahead, going up to Jerusalem. 29When he had come near Bethphage and Bethany, at the place called the Mount of Olives, he sent two of the disciples, 30saying, "Go into the village ahead of you, and as you enter it you will find tied there a colt that has never been ridden. Untie it and bring it here. 31If anyone asks you, 'Why are you untying it?' just say this, 'The Lord needs it.'" 32So those who were sent departed and found it as he had told them. 33As they were untying the colt, its owners asked them, "Why are you untying the colt?" 34They said, "The Lord needs it." 35Then they brought it to Jesus; and after throwing their cloaks on the colt, they set Jesus on it. 36As he rode along, people kept spreading their cloaks on the road. 37As he was now approaching the path down from the Mount of Olives, the whole multitude of the disciples began to praise God joyfully with a loud voice for all the deeds of power that they had seen, 38saying, "Blessed is the king who comes in the name of the Lord! Peace in heaven, and glory in the highest heaven!" 39Some of the Pharisees in the crowd said to him, "Teacher, order your disciples to stop." 40He answered, "I tell you, if these were silent, the stones would shout out."

41As he came near and saw the city, he wept over it, 42saying, "If you, even you, had only recognized on this day the things that make for peace! But now they are hidden from your eyes. 43Indeed, the days will come upon you, when your enemies will set up ramparts around you and surround you, and hem you in on every side. [44]They will crush you to the ground, you and your children within you, and they will not leave within you one stone upon another; because you did not recognize the time of your visitation from God." [45]Then he entered the temple and began to drive out those who were selling things there; [46]and he said, "It is written, 'My house shall be a house of prayer'; but you have made it a den of robbers." [47]Every day he was teaching in the temple. The chief priests, the scribes, and the leaders of the people kept looking for a way to kill him; [48]but they did not find anything they could do, for all the people were spellbound by what they heard.

# Reflection

Even as Jesus is going up to Jerusalem—that is, heading toward his own death—he weeps for us. As Luke's Gospel draws closer to his Passion, the intensity of Jesus' love for humanity burns brighter and brighter. In this passage, great crowds are welcoming Jesus, spreading their cloaks on the ground so that he may enter the city in triumph. But the storm clouds are gathering: both the religious authorities and civic leaders, threatened by his power, are trying to stop Jesus.

Worse, we know that soon even Jesus' disciples, the ones who now do his bidding, will abandon or betray him. The crowds who now hail Jesus as king will turn on him, and the people spellbound by Jesus' teaching will soon deny him. We know that Jesus will be arrested, tortured, mocked, and executed as a criminal. And yet Jesus weeps for us: for our inability to recognize the things that make for peace. It is not the violence we are about to do to Jesus that breaks his heart but our failure to recognize that God is with us.

**Sara Miles**
**Director of Ministry at St. Gregory of Nyssa Episcopal Church**
**San Francisco, California**

## Questions _____

Where in your city or neighborhood do you see Jesus welcomed?

Where do you see him go unrecognized?

## Prayer _____

O God of mercy, break open our hearts of stone, that we may know the time of your visitation and joyfully shout your praise. *Amen.*

## Luke 20:1-47

20 One day, as he was teaching the people in the temple and telling the good news, the chief priests and the scribes came with the elders ²and said to him, "Tell us, by what authority are you doing these things? Who is it who gave you this authority?" ³He answered them, "I will also ask you a question, and you tell me: ⁴Did the baptism of John come from heaven, or was it of human origin?" ⁵They discussed it with one another, saying, "If we say, 'From heaven,' he will say, 'Why did you not believe him?' ⁶But if we say, 'Of human origin,' all the people will stone us; for they are convinced that John was a prophet." ⁷So they answered that they did not know where it came from. ⁸Then Jesus said to them, "Neither will I tell you by what authority I am doing these things."

⁹He began to tell the people this parable: "A man planted a vineyard, and leased it to tenants, and went to another country for a long time. ¹⁰When the season came, he sent a slave to the tenants in order that they might give him his share of the produce of the vineyard; but the tenants beat him and sent him away empty-handed. ¹¹Next he sent another slave; that one also they beat and insulted and sent away empty-handed. ¹²And he sent still a third; this one also they wounded and threw out. ¹³Then the owner of the vineyard said, 'What shall I do? I will send my beloved son; perhaps they will respect him.' ¹⁴But when the tenants saw him, they discussed it among themselves and said, 'This is the heir; let us kill him so that the inheritance may be ours.' ¹⁵So they threw him out of the

vineyard and killed him. What then will the owner of the vineyard do to them? <sup>16</sup>He will come and destroy those tenants and give the vineyard to others." When they heard this, they said, "Heaven forbid!" <sup>17</sup>But he looked at them and said, "What then does this text mean: 'The stone that the builders rejected has become the cornerstone'? <sup>18</sup>Everyone who falls on that stone will be broken to pieces; and it will crush anyone on whom it falls." <sup>19</sup>When the scribes and chief priests realized that he had told this parable against them, they wanted to lay hands on him at that very hour, but they feared the people.

<sup>20</sup>So they watched him and sent spies who pretended to be honest, in order to trap him by what he said, so as to hand him over to the jurisdiction and authority of the governor. <sup>21</sup>So they asked him, "Teacher, we know that you are right in what you say and teach, and you show deference to no one, but teach the way of God in accordance with truth. <sup>22</sup>Is it lawful for us to pay taxes to the emperor, or not?" <sup>23</sup>But he perceived their craftiness and said to them, <sup>24</sup>"Show me a denarius. Whose head and whose title does it bear?" They said, "The emperor's." <sup>25</sup>He said to them, "Then give to the emperor the things that are the emperor's, and to God the things that are God's." <sup>26</sup>And they were not able in the presence of the people to trap him by what he said; and being amazed by his answer, they became silent.

<sup>27</sup>Some Sadducees, those who say there is no resurrection, came to him <sup>28</sup>and asked him a question, "Teacher, Moses wrote for us that if a man's brother dies, leaving a wife but no children, the man shall marry the widow and raise up children for his brother. <sup>29</sup>Now there were seven brothers; the first married, and died childless; <sup>30</sup>then the second <sup>31</sup>and the third married her, and so in the same way all seven died

childless. ³²Finally the woman also died. ³³In the resurrection, therefore, whose wife will the woman be? For the seven had married her." ³⁴Jesus said to them, "Those who belong to this age marry and are given in marriage; ³⁵but those who are considered worthy of a place in that age and in the resurrection from the dead neither marry nor are given in marriage. ³⁶Indeed they cannot die anymore, because they are like angels and are children of God, being children of the resurrection. ³⁷And the fact that the dead are raised Moses himself showed, in the story about the bush, where he speaks of the Lord as the God of Abraham, the God of Isaac, and the God of Jacob. ³⁸Now he is God not of the dead, but of the living; for to him all of them are alive."

³⁹Then some of the scribes answered, "Teacher, you have spoken well." ⁴⁰For they no longer dared to ask him another question. ⁴¹Then he said to them, "How can they say that the Messiah is David's son? ⁴²For David himself says in the book of Psalms, 'The Lord said to my Lord, "Sit at my right hand, ⁴³until I make your enemies your footstool." ' ⁴⁴David thus calls him Lord; so how can he be his son?" ⁴⁵In the hearing of all the people he said to the disciples, ⁴⁶"Beware of the scribes, who like to walk around in long robes, and love to be greeted with respect in the marketplaces, and to have the best seats in the synagogues and places of honor at banquets. ⁴⁷They devour widows' houses and for the sake of appearance say long prayers. They will receive the greater condemnation."

# Reflection

Luke's Gospel grapples frequently with the question of authority: on whose authority, people ask, does Jesus speak and teach and act? Sometimes it's asked as a trick question, as when the chief priests and scribes attempt to trip Jesus up and prove him a *skandalon*, a stumbling stone. Sometimes it's asked with true wonder, as when the centurion, also "a man set under authority," recognizes Jesus as one with unique authority to heal (Luke 7:1-10). But always the questions reveal something about our understanding of the true source of power.

Does authority come from having an imperial army, or a uniform and a gun, or fighter jets? Does it come from owning vast amounts of land and slaves or from being rich beyond measure? Does it come from religion, from building, propping up, and officiating in a temple of stone?

Or does real authority come from God, who only yearns to restore the vineyard of the world to wholeness? Jesus' authority has its source in what the world often rejects as weak, unimportant, and scandalous. It derives from suffering, from forgiveness—and its cornerstone is love.

Sara Miles
Director of Ministry at St. Gregory of Nyssa Episcopal Church
San Francisco, California

## Questions

What is the source of your authority?

How do you reconcile the power of God with the power of the world?

## Prayer

O God our cornerstone and sure foundation, let us not reject your authority, but receive your Son, that we may share the good news of the new world you are building. *Amen.*

## Luke 21:1-38

21 He looked up and saw rich people putting their gifts into the treasury; ²he also saw a poor widow put in two small copper coins. ³He said, "Truly I tell you, this poor widow has put in more than all of them; ⁴for all of them have contributed out of their abundance, but she out of her poverty has put in all she had to live on."

⁵When some were speaking about the temple, how it was adorned with beautiful stones and gifts dedicated to God, he said, ⁶"As for these things that you see, the days will come when not one stone will be left upon another; all will be thrown down." ⁷They asked him, "Teacher, when will this be, and what will be the sign that this is about to take place?" ⁸And he said, "Beware that you are not led astray; for many will come in my name and say, 'I am he!' and, 'The time is near!' Do not go after them. ⁹"When you hear of wars and insurrections, do not be terrified; for these things must take place first, but the end will not follow immediately." ¹⁰Then he said to them, "Nation will rise against nation, and kingdom against kingdom; ¹¹there will be great earthquakes, and in various places famines and plagues; and there will be dreadful portents and great signs from heaven. ¹²"But before all this occurs, they will arrest you and persecute you; they will hand you over to synagogues and prisons, and you will be brought before kings and governors because of my name. ¹³This will give you an opportunity to testify. ¹⁴So make up your minds not to prepare your defense in

advance; <sup>15</sup>for I will give you words and a wisdom that none of your opponents will be able to withstand or contradict. <sup>16</sup>You will be betrayed even by parents and brothers, by relatives and friends; and they will put some of you to death. <sup>17</sup>You will be hated by all because of my name. <sup>18</sup>But not a hair of your head will perish. <sup>19</sup>By your endurance you will gain your souls.

<sup>20</sup>"When you see Jerusalem surrounded by armies, then know that its desolation has come near. <sup>21</sup>Then those in Judea must flee to the mountains, and those inside the city must leave it, and those out in the country must not enter it; <sup>22</sup>for these are days of vengeance, as a fulfillment of all that is written. <sup>23</sup>Woe to those who are pregnant and to those who are nursing infants in those days! For there will be great distress on the earth and wrath against this people; <sup>24</sup>they will fall by the edge of the sword and be taken away as captives among all nations; and Jerusalem will be trampled on by the Gentiles, until the times of the Gentiles are fulfilled. <sup>25</sup>"There will be signs in the sun, the moon, and the stars, and on the earth distress among nations confused by the roaring of the sea and the waves. <sup>26</sup>People will faint from fear and foreboding of what is coming upon the world, for the powers of the heavens will be shaken. <sup>27</sup>Then they will see 'the Son of Man coming in a cloud' with power and great glory. <sup>28</sup>Now when these things begin to take place, stand up and raise your heads, because your redemption is drawing near."

<sup>29</sup>Then he told them a parable: "Look at the fig tree and all the trees; <sup>30</sup>as soon as they sprout leaves you can see for yourselves and know that summer is already near. <sup>31</sup>So also, when you see these things taking place, you know that the kingdom of God is near. <sup>32</sup>Truly I tell you, this generation will not pass away until all things have taken

place. ³³Heaven and earth will pass away, but my words will not pass away. ³⁴"Be on guard so that your hearts are not weighed down with dissipation and drunkenness and the worries of this life, and that day catch you unexpectedly, ³⁵like a trap. For it will come upon all who live on the face of the whole earth. ³⁶Be alert at all times, praying that you may have the strength to escape all these things that will take place, and to stand before the Son of Man." ³⁷Every day he was teaching in the temple, and at night he would go out and spend the night on the Mount of Olives, as it was called. ³⁸And all the people would get up early in the morning to listen to him in the temple.

# Reflection

This text seems out of sync with what we've been reading so far in Luke's Gospel. Here the writing moves into apocalyptic literature with images of catastrophe and destruction and the end of time as we know it. This kind of talk makes most of us nervous and for good reason.

There are always people in the world who embrace apocalyptic thinking by wanting to help usher in the world's destruction rather than its transformation.

While Jesus may have assumed the end of the world as we know it to be more imminent than we do today, his message was always about realizing a new kingdom, God's kingdom, coming to life "on earth as it is in heaven." To be Jesus' disciple is to be engaged in love-transforming acts so that the world will become a fuller reflection of God's love.

And that can involve a reversal of many of our ingrained ways of living. What if we really took to heart our baptismal promises to respect the dignity of every human being—no exceptions, and to seek and serve Christ in all persons—no exceptions? These promises are rooted in the heart of Jesus' vision of the kingdom of God. Imagine how different the world would be if, guided by the Holy Spirit, we made every personal, political, economic, professional, and social decision in light of these promises? The world as we know it would come to an end and the kingdom of God would unfold as a blessing for all of creation. And we would experience life like never before, because we would be living the God-life we were created for in the first place.

**The Rev. Stephen Huber**
**Rector of All Saints' Episcopal Church**
**Beverly Hills, California**

## Questions

How do you understand the call to be Jesus' disciple?

Does this call play out in concrete ways in your life, or is it more of a theological or spiritual concept?

## Prayer

Jesus, I know you experienced times when God did not seem near. But you stayed the course, and in time the glory of God was revealed. Send your Spirit to help me stay the course as your disciple so in time I will come to realize the God-life toward which you are calling me. *Amen.*

## Luke 22:1-23

22 Now the festival of Unleavened Bread, which is called the Passover, was near. ²The chief priests and the scribes were looking for a way to put Jesus to death, for they were afraid of the people. ³Then Satan entered into Judas called Iscariot, who was one of the twelve; ⁴he went away and conferred with the chief priests and officers of the temple police about how he might betray him to them. ⁵They were greatly pleased and agreed to give him money. ⁶So he consented and began to look for an opportunity to betray him to them when no crowd was present.

⁷Then came the day of Unleavened Bread, on which the Passover lamb had to be sacrificed. ⁸So Jesus sent Peter and John, saying, "Go and prepare the Passover meal for us that we may eat it." ⁹They asked him, "Where do you want us to make preparations for it?" ¹⁰"Listen," he said to them, "when you have entered the city, a man carrying a jar of water will meet you; follow him into the house he enters ¹¹and say to the owner of the house, 'The teacher asks you, "Where is the guest room, where I may eat the Passover with my disciples?"' ¹²He will show you a large room upstairs, already furnished. Make preparations for us there." ¹³So they went and found everything as he had told them; and they prepared the Passover meal. ¹⁴When the hour came, he took his place at the table, and the apostles with him. ¹⁵He said to them, "I have eagerly desired to eat this Passover with you before I suffer; ¹⁶for I tell you, I will not eat it until it is fulfilled

in the kingdom of God." [17]Then he took a cup, and after giving thanks he said, "Take this and divide it among yourselves; [18]for I tell you that from now on I will not drink of the fruit of the vine until the kingdom of God comes." [19]Then he took a loaf of bread, and when he had given thanks, he broke it and gave it to them, saying, "This is my body, which is given for you. Do this in remembrance of me." [20]And he did the same with the cup after supper, saying, "This cup that is poured out for you is the new covenant in my blood.

[21]But see, the one who betrays me is with me, and his hand is on the table. [22]For the Son of Man is going as it has been determined, but woe to that one by whom he is betrayed!" [23]Then they began to ask one another, which one of them it could be who would do this.

# Reflection

Every time I read the Old Testament story about God asking Abraham to sacrifice his only son, I cringe. Yet here we are in another difficult story. It is the Last Supper, when things start going south with the news that one in the group will betray Jesus. Suspicion infects the gathering, and we know how the events of the evening unfold. As with Abraham's story, we ask how this squares with our God of love.

But isn't it time that we stop understanding God as the grand puppeteer orchestrating random acts of violence? Rather, in both stories we recognize incredible human faithfulness as well as our worst rationalizations, fears, and weaknesses.

Judas has been cast through the centuries as the evil other one, so beyond the pale and surely not like any of us. If only it were so! The truth is, we veil our betrayals in so many shades of gray.

I want to believe God would have loved nothing more than if Jesus' crucifixion had never happened. Jesus came to reveal the meaning and purpose of life through his life and teaching, but he also discovered that too often we prefer living in the darkness. Nonetheless he was unflinchingly faithful to incarnating God's love, justice, and reconciliation in all that he did. So his earthly life ended on the cross, not because God ordered it, but because we ordered it. His Resurrection affirms the truth of his life and teaching. And in the eucharistic meal, he offers us his life so that we can become his light, his body, in the darkness of our world.

**The Rev. Stephen Huber**
**Rector of All Saints' Episcopal Church**
**Beverly Hills, California**

## Questions

Do you understand the eucharistic banquet as the true body and blood of Christ? How does this understanding impact your daily life and actions?

What is your understanding of the Church as the Body of Christ?

## Prayer

Jesus, help me acknowledge my self-deceptions that keep me from embracing the life you offer. Help me to overcome my fears about entering more fully into the wounds and the joys of the world by giving my life away for the sake of finding it in your love. *Amen.*

## Luke 22:24-46

24A dispute also arose among them as to which one of them was to be regarded as the greatest. 25But he said to them, "The kings of the Gentiles lord it over them; and those in authority over them are called benefactors. 26But not so with you; rather the greatest among you must become like the youngest, and the leader like one who serves. 27For who is greater, the one who is at the table or the one who serves? Is it not the one at the table? But I am among you as one who serves. 28"You are those who have stood by me in my trials; 29and I confer on you, just as my Father has conferred on me, a kingdom, 30so that you may eat and drink at my table in my kingdom, and you will sit on thrones judging the twelve tribes of Israel. 31"Simon, Simon, listen! Satan has demanded to sift all of you like wheat, 32but I have prayed for you that your own faith may not fail; and you, when once you have turned back, strengthen your brothers." 33And he said to him, "Lord, I am ready to go with you to prison and to death!" 34Jesus said, "I tell you, Peter, the cock will not crow this day, until you have denied three times that you know me." 35He said to them, "When I sent you out without a purse, bag, or sandals, did you lack anything?" They said, "No, not a thing." 36He said to them, "But now, the one who has a purse must take it, and likewise a bag. And the one who has no sword must sell his cloak and buy one. 37For I tell you, this scripture must be fulfilled in me, 'And he was counted among the lawless'; and indeed what is written about me is being fulfilled." 38They said, "Lord, look, here are two swords." He replied, "It is enough."

<sup>39</sup>He came out and went, as was his custom, to the Mount of Olives; and the disciples followed him. <sup>40</sup>When he reached the place, he said to them, "Pray that you may not come into the time of trial." <sup>41</sup>Then he withdrew from them about a stone's throw, knelt down, and prayed, <sup>42</sup>"Father, if you are willing, remove this cup from me; yet, not my will but yours be done." <sup>43</sup>Then an angel from heaven appeared to him and gave him strength. <sup>44</sup>In his anguish he prayed more earnestly, and his sweat became like great drops of blood falling down on the ground. <sup>45</sup>When he got up from prayer, he came to the disciples and found them sleeping because of grief, <sup>46</sup>and he said to them, "Why are you sleeping? Get up and pray that you may not come into the time of trial."

# Reflection

I took a history class in college in which the professor opened the course with this searching inquiry: "What makes a great man?" He then listed a variety of historical figures so that we would struggle with the distinctions between greatness, fame, celebrity, and infamy. The Gospel of Luke essentially forces the question of what makes a great disciple. Luke emphasizes the depth of the question by startlingly placing the disciples' dispute over greatness in the midst of the Last Supper.

This narrative of accusation, betrayal, and argument for status positioning is unsettling in contrast to Jesus' teaching and modeling servanthood. A good Bible commentary will reveal the connection between life in the Church and this Last Supper setting. Could it be, the narrative asks, that modern-day disciples struggle and strain for greatness while participating in the discipline of the Lord's Supper with each other?

It is painfully obvious that Jesus repeats himself twice at the Mount of Olives when he tells the disciples, "Pray that you may not come into the time of trial." These words of direction echo the petition in the Lord's Prayer.

What makes a great disciple? The starting point is to recognize that we will have times of trial when we fail to be servants, fail to serve Jesus, and fail to serve one another.

**The Rt. Rev. Dabney T. Smith**
**Bishop of the Diocese of Southwest Florida**
**Parrish, Florida**

## Question _____

Think of a time when you had the opportunity to serve another and intentionally failed to do so. What would you choose to do differently now?

## Prayer _____

Dear Lord, who came not to be served but to serve, you serve me with every breath I take. Help me serve you with my desires, decisions, actions, words, and relationships. You create and love all people. Help me serve those whom you love. This I ask in the name of God the Father, in the love of the Son, and in the power of the Holy Spirit. *Amen.*

## Luke 22:47-71

⁴⁷While he was still speaking, suddenly a crowd came, and the one called Judas, one of the twelve, was leading them. He approached Jesus to kiss him; ⁴⁸but Jesus said to him, "Judas, is it with a kiss that you are betraying the Son of Man?" ⁴⁹When those who were around him saw what was coming, they asked, "Lord, should we strike with the sword?" ⁵⁰Then one of them struck the slave of the high priest and cut off his right ear. ⁵¹But Jesus said, "No more of this!" And he touched his ear and healed him. ⁵²Then Jesus said to the chief priests, the officers of the temple police, and the elders who had come for him, "Have you come out with swords and clubs as if I were a bandit? ⁵³When I was with you day after day in the temple, you did not lay hands on me. But this is your hour, and the power of darkness!"

⁵⁴Then they seized him and led him away, bringing him into the high priest's house. But Peter was following at a distance. ⁵⁵When they had kindled a fire in the middle of the courtyard and sat down together, Peter sat among them. ⁵⁶Then a servant-girl, seeing him in the firelight, stared at him and said, "This man also was with him." ⁵⁷But he denied it, saying, "Woman, I do not know him." ⁵⁸A little later someone else, on seeing him, said, "You also are one of them." But Peter said, "Man, I am not!" ⁵⁹Then about an hour later still another kept insisting, "Surely this man also was with him; for he is a Galilean." ⁶⁰But Peter said, "Man, I do not know what you are talking about!" At that moment, while he was

still speaking, the cock crowed. [61]The Lord turned and looked at Peter. Then Peter remembered the word of the Lord, how he had said to him, "Before the cock crows today, you will deny me three times." [62]And he went out and wept bitterly.

[63]Now the men who were holding Jesus began to mock him and beat him; [64]they also blindfolded him and kept asking him, "Prophesy! Who is it that struck you?" [65]They kept heaping many other insults on him. [66]When day came, the assembly of the elders of the people, both chief priests and scribes, gathered together, and they brought him to their council. [67]They said, "If you are the Messiah, tell us." He replied, "If I tell you, you will not believe; [68]and if I question you, you will not answer. [69]But from now on the Son of Man will be seated at the right hand of the power of God." [70]All of them asked, "Are you, then, the Son of God?" He said to them, "You say that I am." [71]Then they said, "What further testimony do we need? We have heard it ourselves from his own lips!"

# Reflection

Each canonical gospel portrayal of the passion of Jesus offers particular variants in the well-known story. These descriptive elements tell the Jesus story with distinctive nuances, theological frameworks, and character amplifications. Perhaps the most poignant moment in this section of Luke's Gospel lies in the triadic pattern of Peter's denial of relationship with Jesus. At the third vocalization of denial, "...while he was still speaking, the cock crowed. The Lord turned and looked at Peter," Peter recognized the truth about himself, and he went and wept bitterly.

The Lord turned and looked at Peter. What was in the look? Compassion? Knowledge? Disappointment? Love? Worry? The text doesn't tell us. We are only informed of Peter's reaction of shame. This, though, represents the beginning of his transformation from cowardice to courageousness; from disciple to saint. He could not begin the transformation until he metaphorically hit bottom and saw the same truth in himself that the Lord saw.

All of us can understand this moment of the look of the Lord. Any time we deny, or simply gossip about someone, only to discover that person in the room looking at us, we immediately avert our eyes and deny the truth. And the Lord turned and looked at Peter...at Susan, at Charles, at Natalie, at you, at me.

**The Rt. Rev. Dabney T. Smith**
**Bishop of the Diocese of Southwest Florida**
**Parrish, Florida**

## Question

How would the Lord look at you if he saw you today? Remember, if the question strikes you as uncomfortable, perhaps God wants to help transform you from disciple to saint.

## Prayer

Dear Jesus, thank you for loving me. You always see me better than I can possibly see myself. I pray that your gaze upon my soul will remove my guilt, my deceptions, my wounds, and my fears. Look into my life, so that my life may begin to look like yours. This I pray in the holiness of your name. *Amen.*

## Luke 23:1-25

23 Then the assembly rose as a body and brought Jesus before Pilate. ²They began to accuse him, saying, "We found this man perverting our nation, forbidding us to pay taxes to the emperor, and saying that he himself is the Messiah, a king." ³Then Pilate asked him, "Are you the king of the Jews?" He answered, "You say so." ⁴Then Pilate said to the chief priests and the crowds, "I find no basis for an accusation against this man." ⁵But they were insistent and said, "He stirs up the people by teaching throughout all Judea, from Galilee where he began even to this place." ⁶When Pilate heard this, he asked whether the man was a Galilean. ⁷And when he learned that he was under Herod's jurisdiction, he sent him off to Herod, who was himself in Jerusalem at that time. ⁸When Herod saw Jesus, he was very glad, for he had been wanting to see him for a long time, because he had heard about him and was hoping to see him perform some sign. ⁹He questioned him at some length, but Jesus gave him no answer. ¹⁰The chief priests and the scribes stood by, vehemently accusing him. ¹¹Even Herod with his soldiers treated him with contempt and mocked him; then he put an elegant robe on him, and sent him back to Pilate. ¹²That same day Herod and Pilate became friends with each other; before this they had been enemies.

¹³Pilate then called together the chief priests, the leaders, and the people, ¹⁴and said to them, "You brought me this man as one who was perverting the people; and here I have examined him in your presence and have not

found this man guilty of any of your charges against him. [15]Neither has Herod, for he sent him back to us. Indeed, he has done nothing to deserve death. [16]I will therefore have him flogged and release him." [18]Then they all shouted out together, "Away with this fellow! Release Barabbas for us!" [19](This was a man who had been put in prison for an insurrection that had taken place in the city, and for murder.) [20]Pilate, wanting to release Jesus, addressed them again; [21]but they kept shouting, "Crucify, crucify him!" [22]A third time he said to them, "Why, what evil has he done? I have found in him no ground for the sentence of death; I will therefore have him flogged and then release him." [23]But they kept urgently demanding with loud shouts that he should be crucified; and their voices prevailed. [24]So Pilate gave his verdict that their demand should be granted. [25]He released the man they asked for, the one who had been put in prison for insurrection and murder, and he handed Jesus over as they wished.

# Reflection

Were this not such a sobering scene, we might imagine Jesus as the hot potato. No one wants to be held accountable for his death. Following the Sanhedrin trial, the assembly brings Jesus before Pontius Pilate, prefect of Rome's Judean province. Finding him guilty of no crime, Pilate sends Jesus back to his local jurisdiction, headed by Herod Antipas. Herod, who has been waiting a long time to meet Jesus, can't wait to pass him back to Pilate and avoid the wrath of the crowd.

Finally Pilate washes his hands of any responsibility for the bloodthirsty crowd who demand Jesus' execution. If they want him crucified, even instead of the proven, hardened criminal Barabbas, they can have him. By the end of this scene, Luke makes it clear that everyone rejects Jesus. His blood is on all their hands.

In this shirking of responsibility, the worst tendencies of people pressed into a crowd mentality arise: they convict the innocent, torment the victim, pass the buck on responsibility, capitulate to peer pressure, and forge once unthinkable alliances out of mutual disdain.

In a grand episode of scapegoating, those who take no direct action stand by and let calamity unfold. The common people hide behind the politicians and religious authorities. The authorities hide behind the rules. The soldiers hide behind their orders. Everyone succumbs to the momentum of a deeply tragic trajectory. Most troubling, no one stands up for Jesus, and he doesn't even stand up for himself. He goes to his death—a lamb led to the slaughter.

**The Rev. Christine T. McSpadden**
**Clergy at St. Paul's Cathedral**
**London, England**

## Questions _____

Why do you think Jesus stands by, puts himself at the mercy of events as they unfold, and does not stand up for himself?

Can you think of a situation where you have stood by and watched as a tragic situation unfolded without intervening to stop it?

## Prayer _____

Reconciling God, we offer to you our betrayals and defeats, our excuses and eagerness to blame. As we lay before you what we have done, pardon who we are, and direct who we shall be. May our hearts be filled with delight for your invitation to repent and return. *Amen.*

## Luke 23:26-43

<sup>26</sup>As they led him away, they seized a man, Simon of Cyrene, who was coming from the country, and they laid the cross on him, and made him carry it behind Jesus. <sup>27</sup>A great number of the people followed him, and among them were women who were beating their breasts and wailing for him. <sup>28</sup>But Jesus turned to them and said, "Daughters of Jerusalem, do not weep for me, but weep for yourselves and for your children. <sup>29</sup>For the days are surely coming when they will say, 'Blessed are the barren, and the wombs that never bore, and the breasts that never nursed.' <sup>30</sup>Then they will begin to say to the mountains, 'Fall on us'; and to the hills, 'Cover us.' <sup>31</sup>For if they do this when the wood is green, what will happen when it is dry?"

<sup>32</sup>Two others also, who were criminals, were led away to be put to death with him. <sup>33</sup>When they came to the place that is called The Skull, they crucified Jesus there with the criminals, one on his right and one on his left. <sup>34</sup>Then Jesus said, "Father, forgive them; for they do not know what they are doing." And they cast lots to divide his clothing. <sup>35</sup>And the people stood by, watching; but the leaders scoffed at him, saying, "He saved others; let him save himself if he is the Messiah of God, his chosen one!" <sup>36</sup>The soldiers also mocked him, coming up and offering him sour wine, <sup>37</sup>and saying, "If you are the King of the Jews, save yourself!" <sup>38</sup>There was also an inscription over him, "This is the King of the Jews." <sup>39</sup>One of the criminals who were

hanged there kept deriding him and saying, "Are you not the Messiah? Save yourself and us!" [40]But the other rebuked him, saying, "Do you not fear God, since you are under the same sentence of condemnation? [41]And we indeed have been condemned justly, for we are getting what we deserve for our deeds, but this man has done nothing wrong." [42]Then he said, "Jesus, remember me when you come into your kingdom." [43]He replied, "Truly I tell you, today you will be with me in Paradise."

# Reflection

In the events surrounding Jesus' death as described by Luke in this passage, two movements emerge: The first movement is the *via dolorosa*, the way of the cross, described in these verses. The second is the actual crucifixion scene, the events surrounding the execution of Jesus at Calvary. Throughout the events comprising these movements, Luke draws a sharp contrast between the cruelty of mortals and the compassion of God. Consistently, as Jesus carries his cross to the Place of the Skull and, consequently, his own death, he never stops engaging with people and ministering to them along the way; he even continues his ministrations from the cross.

Luke's Gospel includes material absent from other accounts— most notably Jesus' words of warning to the women of Jerusalem, prophesying the unpleasant things to come for the nation of Israel in general, and for those who live in Jerusalem specifically, Jesus' words of acceptance and absolution from the cross, "Father, forgive them; for they do not know what they are doing" and his invitation to the thief on the cross to join him in paradise. In each case, even as he is dehumanized himself, Jesus reaches out to those around him from a place of humanity and humility with an undying disposition of concern, compurgation, and communion. In each case, he shifts the focus away from his suffering to embrace their suffering.

**The Rev. Christine T. McSpadden**
**Clergy at St. Paul's Cathedral**
**London, England**

## Questions

How does the contrast between humanity's cruelty and God's compassion serve the larger message of Luke's Gospel?

What is the significance of Luke's telling us that Simon is from Cyrene?

## Prayer

Compassionate God, we pray for those whose lives are filled with darkness and emptiness, whose souls are filled with despair. We pray for those too afraid, disillusioned, or despondent to even consider the future. Give them the will to cope and the grace to hope, through the compassion and mercy of Jesus. *Amen.*

## Luke 23:44-56

⁴⁴It was now about noon, and darkness came over the whole land until three in the afternoon, ⁴⁵while the sun's light failed; and the curtain of the temple was torn in two. ⁴⁶Then Jesus, crying with a loud voice, said, "Father, into your hands I commend my spirit." Having said this, he breathed his last. ⁴⁷When the centurion saw what had taken place, he praised God and said, "Certainly this man was innocent." ⁴⁸And when all the crowds who had gathered there for this spectacle saw what had taken place, they returned home, beating their breasts. ⁴⁹But all his acquaintances, including the women who had followed him from Galilee, stood at a distance, watching these things.

⁵⁰Now there was a good and righteous man named Joseph, who, though a member of the council, ⁵¹had not agreed to their plan and action. He came from the Jewish town of Arimathea, and he was waiting expectantly for the kingdom of God. ⁵²This man went to Pilate and asked for the body of Jesus. ⁵³Then he took it down, wrapped it in a linen cloth, and laid it in a rock-hewn tomb where no one had ever been laid. ⁵⁴It was the day of Preparation, and the sabbath was beginning. ⁵⁵The women who had come with him from Galilee followed, and they saw the tomb and how his body was laid. ⁵⁶Then they returned, and prepared spices and ointments. On the sabbath they rested according to the commandment.

# Reflection

This section of Luke's Gospel is about the death and burial of Jesus, yes, but in a real way, it is about those who witnessed these things. It's about the centurion who might have been convicted by his participation in the death of an innocent man. It's about the bystanders, including Jesus' own friends, who stood at a safe distance and after the spectacle went home, sobered and sickened. It's about Joseph of Arimathea, a perhaps pious and apparently well-off admirer of Jesus who provides a decent grave for his body. It's about the women who took note of where the tomb was so that they could come back and provide the customary washing and anointing of the corpse.

This story is about you and me.

It is sometimes said that the Bible's account of the death and resurrection of Jesus is less a story about what happened to him than it is a story about what happened to his friends, about what continues to happen to them. It is about what happens to women and men when they move from merely observing these things to encountering them. The gospel is the mighty good news of what happens to us when we meet the dying and rising Jesus in our lives, when we hear him calling our name, when we trust him with our own dying and rising. The story of Jesus is still the story of the members of his body.

**The Rt. Rev. Jeffrey D. Lee**
**Bishop of the Diocese of Chicago**
**Chicago, Illinois**

## Question _____

When have you encountered the dying and rising of Jesus?

## Prayer _____

Lord Jesus Christ, you love us even when we insist on standing at a safe distance from your agony. Strengthen us to come close to you, to embrace your death and all the deaths of our world, confident that you have opened a way through death to new and unimaginable life beyond. *Amen.*

## Luke 24:1-12

24 But on the first day of the week, at early dawn, they came to the tomb, taking the spices that they had prepared. ²They found the stone rolled away from the tomb, ³but when they went in, they did not find the body. ⁴While they were perplexed about this, suddenly two men in dazzling clothes stood beside them. ⁵The women were terrified and bowed their faces to the ground, but the men said to them, "Why do you look for the living among the dead? He is not here, but has risen. ⁶Remember how he told you, while he was still in Galilee, ⁷that the Son of Man must be handed over to sinners, and be crucified, and on the third day rise again." ⁸Then they remembered his words, ⁹and returning from the tomb, they told all this to the eleven and to all the rest. ¹⁰Now it was Mary Magdalene, Joanna, Mary the mother of James, and the other women with them who told this to the apostles. ¹¹But these words seemed to them an idle tale, and they did not believe them. ¹²But Peter got up and ran to the tomb; stooping and looking in, he saw the linen cloths by themselves; then he went home, amazed at what had happened.

# Reflection

The biblical accounts of the Resurrection of Jesus all take place sometime before dawn when there was no one to see what actually happened. There are no eyewitnesses of this mystery we call resurrection. That is an important truth. Resurrection is not something you can see or measure or capture or even describe. It is something you have to enter, to experience, something you have to allow to grasp you. The only thing there is to describe about resurrection is what results from it—new life. The Bible's accounts are profoundly truthful.

There is a cosmic dimension to the Resurrection—in the Risen Christ all creation begins to be made new. And there is a personal dimension not unrelated to this. In the Risen Christ I am made new, again and again. One of my favorite Easter hymns puts it like this: "When our hearts are wintry, grieving or in pain, thy touch can call us back to life again." By God's design the earth itself displays the evidence of new life emerging from death, and by God's grace so can our lives. Right here. Right now. Resurrection isn't something we have to wait for, some day, in the sweet by and by. It isn't only something that happens at the end of time. It is waiting to happen now in the daily realities of our relationships, our work, our tears, and our joys. Love has conquered death. Alleluia.

**The Rt. Rev. Jeffrey D. Lee**
**Bishop of the Diocese of Chicago**
**Chicago, Illinois**

## Question

Where do you see evidence of resurrection?

## Prayer

Holy and life-giving God, your love creates all things, sustains all things, and holds all of it in your deathless embrace. Open our eyes, our hearts, our lives to your presence that we may recognize the Risen One who stands among us, closer than our next breath, your Son Jesus Christ, who lives and reigns with you and the Holy Spirit, one God, now and forever. *Amen.*

## Luke 24:13-35

¹³Now on that same day two of them were going to a village called Emmaus, about seven miles from Jerusalem, ¹⁴and talking with each other about all these things that had happened. ¹⁵While they were talking and discussing, Jesus himself came near and went with them, ¹⁶but their eyes were kept from recognizing him. ¹⁷And he said to them, "What are you discussing with each other while you walk along?" They stood still, looking sad. ¹⁸Then one of them, whose name was Cleopas, answered him, "Are you the only stranger in Jerusalem who does not know the things that have taken place there in these days?" ¹⁹He asked them, "What things?" They replied, "The things about Jesus of Nazareth, who was a prophet mighty in deed and word before God and all the people, ²⁰and how our chief priests and leaders handed him over to be condemned to death and crucified him. ²¹But we had hoped that he was the one to redeem Israel. Yes, and besides all this, it is now the third day since these things took place. ²²Moreover, some women of our group astounded us. They were at the tomb early this morning, ²³and when they did not find his body there, they came back and told us that they had indeed seen a vision of angels who said that he was alive. ²⁴Some of those who were with us went to the tomb and found it just as the women had said; but they did not see him." ²⁵Then he said to them, "Oh, how foolish you are, and how slow of heart to believe all that the prophets have declared! ²⁶Was it not necessary that the Messiah should suffer these things and then enter into his

glory?" <sup>27</sup>Then beginning with Moses and all the prophets, he interpreted to them the things about himself in all the scriptures. <sup>28</sup>As they came near the village to which they were going, he walked ahead as if he were going on. <sup>29</sup>But they urged him strongly, saying, "Stay with us, because it is almost evening and the day is now nearly over." So he went in to stay with them. <sup>30</sup>When he was at the table with them, he took bread, blessed and broke it, and gave it to them. <sup>31</sup>Then their eyes were opened, and they recognized him; and he vanished from their sight. <sup>32</sup>They said to each other, "Were not our hearts burning within us while he was talking to us on the road, while he was opening the scriptures to us?" <sup>33</sup>That same hour they got up and returned to Jerusalem; and they found the eleven and their companions gathered together. <sup>34</sup>They were saying, "The Lord has risen indeed, and he has appeared to Simon!" <sup>35</sup>Then they told what had happened on the road, and how he had been made known to them in the breaking of the bread.

# Reflection

This whole passage is about (mis)recognition—about who knows what and how.

These two disciples at first suppose that their travel companion is the one in the dark. They know "the things that have taken place;" he apparently does not. But while they know what has happened, their companion knows what it all means.

They might have put it together, we suppose. The mention that "it is now the third day since these things took place" is almost too obvious; Jesus had told them what was to happen on the third day (9:22, 13:32, 18:33). The companion voices our frustration: how could these guys not understand? And then he explains everything to them.

But even then, this is not how the Son of Man is recognized. Not with clues and a mystery pieced together. It's not about knowing what happened; it's not about figuring it out.

Jesus is seen only when he disappears. Again and again, it's those who can't see Jesus who truly recognize him: the women at the tomb who cannot find the body, those who follow on "but did not see him."

The pattern repeats itself again. The companion takes bread, blesses and breaks it, and gives it to them. Their eyes are opened, they recognize him, and he vanishes from their sight.

From now on, he is the one made known in the breaking of the bread—in the table fellowship of the church, in the Eucharist.

**Miroslav Volf**
**Henry B. Wright Professor of Systematic Theology**
**at Yale Divinity School**
**New Haven, Connecticut**

## Questions

How is Jesus made known to you in the breaking of the bread—in the communal life of the church, in particular in the Eucharist?

How is this mysterious revelation of Jesus different from mere facts you can know about Jesus?

## Prayer

Mysterious Lord, we thank you for being made known to us in the breaking of the bread. Reveal yourself to us in our life together. May we truly discern the Body of Christ and be formed in Christ's likeness. *Amen.*

## Luke 24:36-53

³⁶While they were talking about this, Jesus himself stood among them and said to them, "Peace be with you." ³⁷They were startled and terrified, and thought that they were seeing a ghost. ³⁸He said to them, "Why are you frightened, and why do doubts arise in your hearts? ³⁹Look at my hands and my feet; see that it is I myself. Touch me and see; for a ghost does not have flesh and bones as you see that I have." ⁴⁰And when he had said this, he showed them his hands and his feet. ⁴¹While in their joy they were disbelieving and still wondering, he said to them, "Have you anything here to eat?" ⁴²They gave him a piece of broiled fish, ⁴³and he took it and ate in their presence. ⁴⁴Then he said to them, "These are my words that I spoke to you while I was still with you—

that everything written about me in the law of Moses, the prophets, and the psalms must be fulfilled." ⁴⁵Then he opened their minds to understand the scriptures, ⁴⁶and he said to them, "Thus it is written, that the Messiah is to suffer and to rise from the dead on the third day, ⁴⁷and that repentance and forgiveness of sins is to be proclaimed in his name to all nations, beginning from Jerusalem. ⁴⁸You are witnesses of these things. ⁴⁹And see, I am sending upon you what my Father promised; so stay here in the city until you have been clothed with power from on high."

⁵⁰Then he led them out as far as Bethany, and, lifting up his hands, he blessed them. ⁵¹While he was blessing them, he withdrew from them and

was carried up into heaven. [52]And they worshiped him, and returned to Jerusalem with great joy; [53]and they were continually in the temple blessing God.

# Reflection

And so ends the Gospel of Luke, the gospel of joy. Luke begins and ends in joy.

Jesus' entrance into Jerusalem is greeted with joy on Palm Sunday, as is Judas' offer to betray him. Joy, it seems, is not above the possibility of perversion. We can be wrong about joy; we can pursue it in the wrong place. As a result, pursuing joy alone isn't a method for seeking the kingdom.

In fact, the pursuit of joy itself may be impossible. In Luke, joy isn't something we pursue. Rather, joy pursues us. Joy surprises us. It attends the birth of a child both long-awaited and yet nevertheless profoundly surprising. It shines through even the hardship of persecution. It attends the unexpected discovery of lost treasure, the repentance of a sinner, and the barely-imaginable return of the long-lost son. Joy startles us in the savior's scandalous pursuit of the sinner, Zacchaeus.

And, in the end, after that savior has died for us and yet also at our hands (Acts 2:23), joy attends the shocking revelation that this savior is nevertheless pursuing us in love. Not even our enmity—not even the grave—can hold him back. And so, as Luke ends and Acts begins, we are sent out as his witnesses—to joy.

**Matthew Croasmun**
**Lecturer of Theology and Humanities at Yale University**
**New Haven, Connecticut**

## Questions

How have you been surprised by the good news? How have you experienced the joy of God's loving pursuit? How might you live as a witness of that joy?

## Prayer

God of love and giver of joy, we thank you for the fact that your love pursues us, even in the face of our sin and our opposition to your work. Let us not rejoice in evil but rather rejoice in the truth. Surprise us with your joy and send us out as witnesses to that joy. *Amen.*

# ABOUT THE AUTHORS

**J. Neil Alexander** is a bishop of The Episcopal Church and presently serves as the dean of the School of Theology of the University of the South, Sewanee, Tennessee. He is also a professor of liturgy and Charles Todd Quintard Professor of Dogmatic Theology. Prior to that, he served as bishop of the Diocese of Atlanta and professor of liturgics at the General Theological Seminary. (Days 5, 6)

**Marjorie Brown** served a curacy in the East End of London and worked for ten years as a parish priest in a vibrant Hackney community with Muslim and Hasidic Jewish neighbors. She is now the vicar of St. Mary's Primrose Hill, where Percy Dearmer famously set new standards in congregational music and liturgical practice a century ago. She is also one of the directors of ordinands in the Diocese of London. (Days 21, 22)

**Matthew Croasmun** is lecturer of theology and humanities at Yale University and the director of research and publication at the Yale Center for Faith & Culture. In 2007, he helped plant the Elm City Vineyard Church, where he currently serves as a staff pastor. His Yale dissertation, "The Body of Sin," was awarded the 2015 Manfred Lautenschläger Award for Theological Promise. (Day 50)

**Robert S. Dannals** became the seventh rector of Saint Michael and All Angels Church in Dallas, Texas, in 2007. A graduate of Florida State University (BA in Religion) and Virginia Theological Seminary (M.Div.), he served churches in North and South Carolina prior to his move to Dallas. He also received his D.Min. from Drew University and a doctorate in practical theology from Graduate Theological Union, writing his dissertation on Dietrich Bonhoeffer.

A north Florida native, he is married to Valerie, and they have three adult daughters. (Days 29, 30)

**MIGUEL ESCOBAR** is senior program director of leadership resources at the Episcopal Church Foundation (ECF). A lay person, he is passionate about building the next generation of lay and clergy leaders in The Episcopal Church. He received his M.Div. from Union Theological Seminary in 2007. (Days 17, 18)

**VICKI GARVEY** serves as bishop's associate for lifelong Christian formation in the Episcopal Diocese of Chicago. Passionate about learning and teaching, she has taught at nearly every level from second graders through graduate school, but she has spent most of that teaching time at Bexley Hall Seabury Western Seminary Federation where she taught biblical languages and biblical theology. She is a popular speaker and workshop leader and serves the wider church as board member and committee member of several churchwide commissions and a deputy to General Convention. (Days 33, 34)

**SCOTT HAYASHI** is the eleventh bishop of the Episcopal Diocese of Utah. He has contributed essays to collections published by The Episcopal Church. He has served in congregations large and small and was the canon to the ordinary in the Diocese of Chicago prior to his election as a bishop. Bishop Hayashi has written more than 750 daily Bible reflections that are posted to Facebook. He has extensive experience working with clergy through ten years as a conference leader for CREDO. (Days 13, 14)

**STEPHEN HUBER** is rector of All Saints' Parish in Beverly Hills, California. He served previously as the vicar of Washington National Cathedral, priest-in-charge of St. Columba's Church, Washington, DC, and development director of Berkeley Divinity School at Yale.

For ten years, he taught religious studies on the secondary school level in New Orleans and Boston, and for thirteen years, he worked in nonprofit advocacy fundraising for HIV/AIDS and LGBT human rights in Boston and Washington, DC. (Days 41, 42)

**MIKE KINMAN** is the dean of Christ Church Cathedral in St. Louis, Missouri, and the board president of Magdalene St. Louis, a two-year residential community of loving healing for women who have survived lives of prostitution, violence, and abuse. Michael lives with his wife, Robin, and sons, Schroedter and Hayden, in St. Louis. (Days 25, 26)

**JEFFREY D. LEE** has served since 2008 as the twelfth bishop of the Episcopal Diocese of Chicago. He leads 40,000 Episcopalians in 124 congregations across Northern Illinois. A charismatic preacher, liturgist, and spiritual leader, he is committed to helping the congregations of the diocese grow the church, form the faithful, and change the world. He is the author of *Opening the Prayer Book* in the New Church's Teaching Series; a member of the Board of Directors of Episcopal Relief & Development; a former member of the faculty of CREDO Institute; and has served on the board of Affirming Catholicism. He and his wife, Lisa Rogers Lee, have two children, Katherine and Jonathan. (Days 47, 48)

**RUSSELL LEVENSON JR.** and his wife, Laura, live in Houston, Texas, where Russ serves as rector of St. Martin's Episcopal Church. He has written widely for various publications and religious journals, and is the author of three books, *Provoking Thoughts* (a Lenten meditation book); *Preparing Room* (an Advent meditation book), and *Summer Times* (a devotional book for the summer). He and Laura have also written two Advent wreath devotional guides, one for adults and one for children. (Days 37, 38)

**Edward S. Little II** has served as bishop of the Episcopal Diocese of Northern Indiana since 2000. His earlier assignments include parishes in the dioceses of Chicago, Los Angeles, and San Joaquin. A graduate of the University of Southern California and Seabury-Western Theological Seminary, Bishop Little and his wife, Sylvia, are the parents of Gregory and Sharon and the grandparents of Taj and Lani. (Days 23, 24)

**William Lupfer** is rector of Trinity Wall Street. He has been a parish priest for twenty-one years, serving in Oregon, Michigan, and Illinois. His focus has been on parish leadership development as a process of spiritual formation. He has been married to Kimiko Koga for twenty-five years. They have two children. (Days 1, 2)

**John M. McCardell Jr.** is vice-chancellor and president of The University of the South, Sewanee, Tennessee, where he has served since 2010. A historian by training and winner of the Allan Nevins Prize for his book, *The Idea of a Southern Nation,* he joined the faculty of Middlebury College, Middlebury, Vermont, in 1976 and served as president of the college from 1991 to 2004. He is a graduate of Washington and Lee University and earned his Ph.D. at Harvard University. (Days 27, 28)

**Andrew B. McGowan** is dean of the Berkeley Divinity School and McFaddin Professor of Anglican Studies at Yale. He is the author of *Ancient Christian Worship* and blogs at Saint Ronan Street Diary (abmcg.blogspot.com). (Days 31, 32)

**Christine T. McSpadden** is a graduate of the University of Virginia and Berkeley Divinity School at Yale and has served in congregations from New York City to San Francisco. She currently lives in London, England where she is a member of the clergy team of St. Paul's Cathedral. (Days 45, 46)

**Sara Miles** is the author of *Take This Bread, Jesus Freak: Feeding Healing Raising the Dead*, and *City of God: Faith in the Streets*. She is the director of ministry at St. Gregory of Nyssa Episcopal Church in San Francisco, California. (Days 39, 40)

**Kate Moorehead** is the dean of St. John's Cathedral in Jacksonville, Florida. She is the author of four books: *Between Two Worlds, Organic God, Get Over Yourself: God's Here!* and *Resurrecting Easter*. Kate is married to JD Moorehead, a psychotherapist, and they have three boys. (Days 15, 16)

**C. K. Robertson** serves as canon to the presiding bishop as well as distinguished visiting professor at General Theological Seminary in New York City. An active member of the Council on Foreign Relations and the National Council of Churches, and a fellow of the Episcopal Church Foundation, Robertson is general editor of the *Studies in Episcopal and Anglican Theology* series, and author of many books. His most recent book is *Barnabas vs. Paul: To Encourage or Confront*. (Days 19, 20)

**Matthew Sleeth, MD,** has spoken at more than 1,000 churches, campuses, and events, including serving as a monthly guest preacher at the Washington National Cathedral. Recognized by *Newsweek* as one of the nation's most influential evangelical leaders, Sleeth is the executive director of Blessed Earth, an educational nonprofit focused on stewardship of the earth. He is the founder of the Seminary Stewardship Alliance and author of numerous books and articles. (Days 11, 12)

**DABNEY T. SMITH** is the fifth bishop of the Episcopal Diocese of Southwest Florida. Before election as bishop he served in the dioceses of Central Florida, Northern Indiana, and Louisiana. Dabney and his wife, Mary, have five adult children and six wonderful grandchildren. (Days 43, 44)

**MARTIN L. SMITH** is well-known throughout The Episcopal Church and beyond as a preacher, teacher, and retreat leader. His explorations of contemporary spirituality have been made accessible to a wide readership in such books as *The Word is Very Near You, A Season for the Spirit, Reconciliation, Love Set Free,* and *Compass and Stars.* He resides in Washington, DC, and travels widely in his ministry of spiritual formation. (Days 7, 8)

**GREGORY E. STERLING** is the Reverend Henry L. Slack Dean and the Lillian Claus Professor of New Testament at Yale Divinity School. He is a recognized expert in the study of Luke-Acts, Josephus, and Philo of Alexandria. He is an ordained minister in Churches of Christ and has served churches in several states. (Days 3, 4)

**DAME MARY TANNER** is a world-renowned ecumenist. Before retirement, she served as the general secretary of the Church of England's Council for Christian Unity. A lay theologian, she was a member of the Faith and Order Commission of the World Council of Churches and its moderator from 1991-1998, a member of the Anglican-Roman Catholic International Commission, and the president for Europe of the World Council of Churches. She has been a visiting professor at the General Theological Seminary in New York City, the Tantur Ecumenical Institute in Jerusalem, and the Pontifical University of Saint Thomas Aquinas in Rome. (Days 9, 10)

**MIROSLAV VOLF** is Henry B. Wright Professor of Systematic Theology at Yale Divinity School and the founding director of the Yale Center for Faith & Culture. He has written or edited more than seventy scholarly articles and fifteen books, including *Exclusion and Embrace* (1996, winner of the 2002 Grawemeyer Award), *A Public Faith: On How Followers of Christ Should Serve the Common Good* (2011), and *Allah: A Christian Response* (2011). He is actively involved in many top-level initiatives concerning Christian-Muslim relations and is a member of the Global Agenda Council of the World Economic Forum. (Day 49)

**JESSE ZINK** is a priest of the Diocese of Western Massachusetts and a doctoral student and assistant chaplain at Emmanuel College, Cambridge University, where his research focuses on the church in southern Sudan. He is a former Young Adult Service Corps missionary and the author of *Backpacking through the Anglican Communion: A Search for Unity.* (Days 35, 36)

**Marek P. Zabriskie** has served as rector of St. Thomas' Episcopal Church in Fort Washington, Pennsylvania, since 1995. Prior to that he served churches in Nashville, Tennessee, and Richmond, Virginia. In 2011, he founded The Bible Challenge, which has spread to over 2,500 churches in more than fifty countries with over 500,000 persons participating. He is the editor of several books, including *The Bible Challenge* published by Forward Movement and *Doing the Bible Better: The Bible Challenge and the Transformation of The Episcopal Church.*

## ABOUT FORWARD MOVEMENT

Forward Movement is committed to inspiring disciples and empowering evangelists. While we produce great resources like this book, Forward Movement is not a publishing company. We are a ministry.

Our mission is to support you in your spiritual journey, to help you grow as a follower of Jesus Christ. Publishing books, daily reflections, studies for small groups, and online resources is an important way that we live out this ministry. More than a half million people read our daily devotions through *Forward Day by Day*, which is also available in Spanish (*Adelante Día a Día*) and Braille, online, as a podcast, and as an app for your smartphones or tablets. It is mailed to more than fifty countries, and we donate nearly 30,000 copies each quarter to prisons, hospitals, and nursing homes. We actively seek partners across the Church and look for ways to provide resources that inspire and challenge.

A ministry of The Episcopal Church for eighty years, Forward Movement is a nonprofit organization funded by sales of resources and gifts from generous donors. To learn more about Forward Movement and our resources, please visit us at www.forwardmovement.org (or www.adelanteenelcamino.org).

We are delighted to be doing this work and invite your prayers and support.